VICTORY IN EUROPE

VICTORY IN EUROPE

THE ALLIES' DEFEAT OF THE AXIS FORCES

KAREN FARRINGTON

This edition published in 2020 by Arcturus Publishing Limited
26/27 Bickels Yard, 151–153 Bermondsey Street,
London SE1 3HA

ISBN: 978-1-83940-269-2
AD000457UK

Printed in China

CONTENTS

Introduction

'The future of the war is in our hands.'

Homer, The Iliad

Few people alive today can claim to have witnessed the frantic, sodden dashes from surf to dune, the cratered sandscape, the sooty sea air and the wild-eyed adrenalin that was D-Day, the military operation that enabled the Allies to force their way back into mainland Europe having been unceremoniously evicted by Hitler's forces in the early stages of the Second World War.

The battalions of soldiers who crouched on landing craft, silently praying for a swift passage to the far side of the sands on the Normandy beaches, are rapidly diminishing. Those airmen who terrorised Wehrmacht positions, immeasurably assisting advancing troops, are fewer in number each year. Many of the sailors who, at huge risk, helped ferry invading forces across the English channel have died in the intervening sixty years since D-Day. Paratroopers who called on hitherto unknown reserves of personal courage as they were dropped behind enemy lines are likewise dwindling in number. Only one in five Germans alive today experienced the traumas of the Second World War. There were very many, of course, of numerous nationalities who did not survive to tell the tale.

Yet the courage of all these men who refused to be thrown back into the sea, not to mention the audacity of the military planners, is a recurring topic even in the 21st century. This multitude of heroes fought for the noble principle of freedom and that helps them loom large in the collective consciousness.

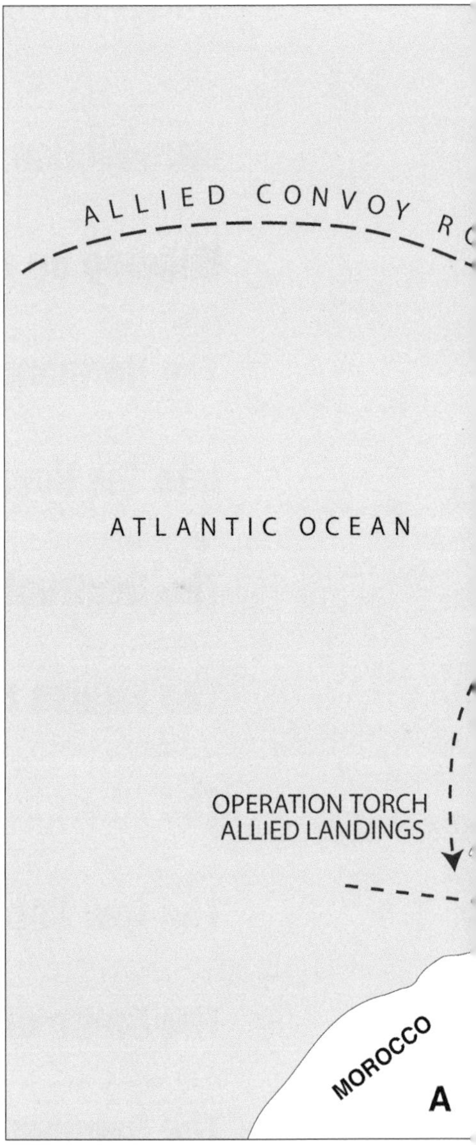

This is breathless history. It was as much an assault on the senses as on German-held France and most of us can vividly imagine

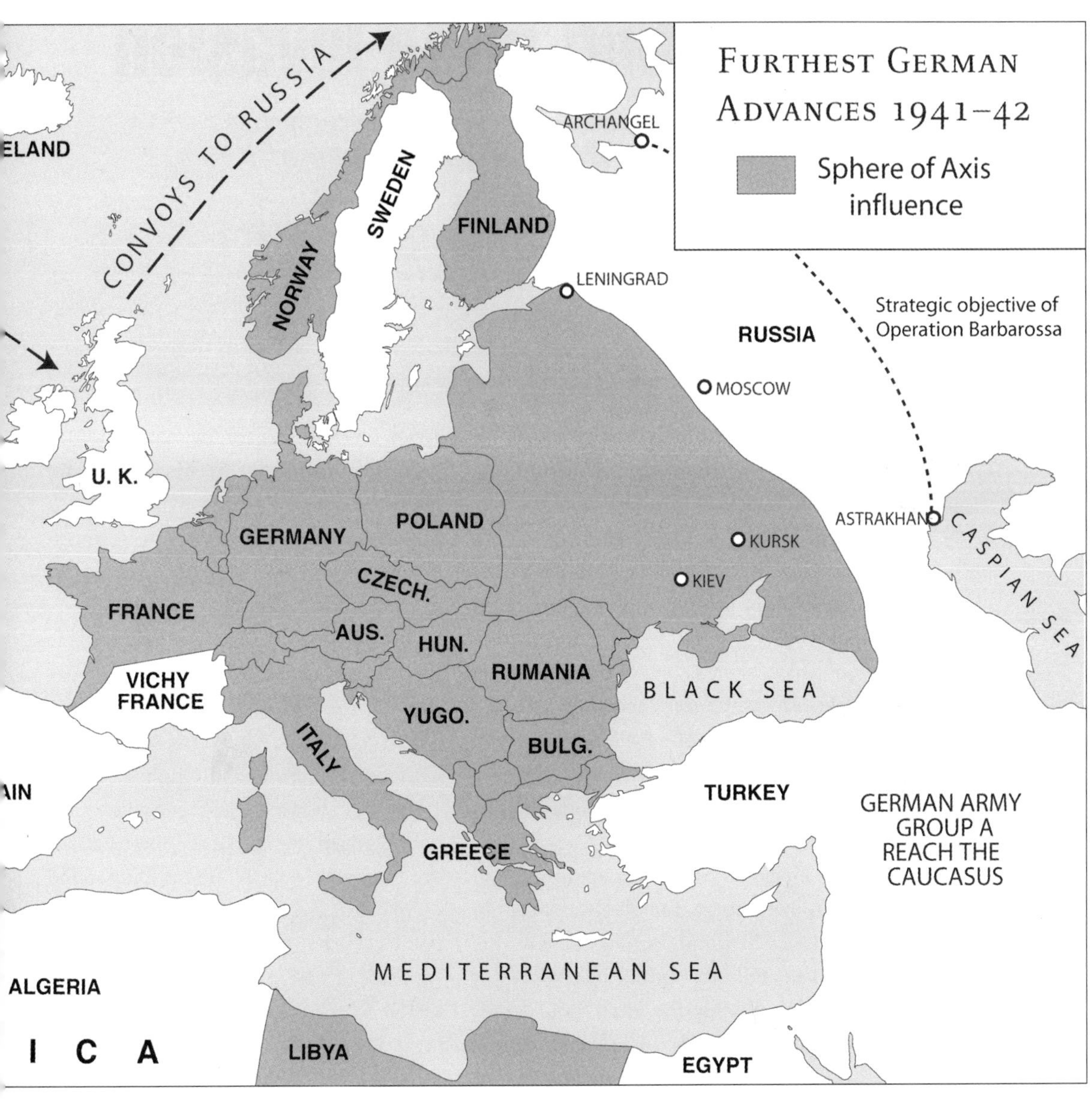

the array of sights, the barrage of sounds, the taste of fear and the odour of impassioned warfare. This book aims to provide a reference for those who may have difficulty in summoning up relevant or accurate images. Crucially, it goes beyond D-Day and its immediate aftermath. D-Day indeed put the Allies on the road to victory but it was by no means decisive. The German grip on the European continent may have been loosened, but it would take almost another year of gruelling fighting before the final order of surrender of all German arms was signed by Grand Admiral Karl Dönitz, leader of a broken nation after Hitler's suicide in his Berlin bunker on 30 April 1945. *Victory in Europe* is the story of those final gruelling months of the European theatre of the Second World War.

Evil Empire
Map showing the furthest extent of the Nazi Third Reich, circa 1942.

CHAPTER ONE

Building up to Invasion

'This war will be won or lost on the beaches'

Field Marshal Gerd von Rundstedt, June 1944

With hindsight, it seems inevitable that once the Allies had a foothold in Normandy, they would blithely roll through France, into Germany and straight to the heart of the Third Reich, ending Hitler's boast of a thousand-year reign. In fact, the advance could have stalled, or even been thrown back, on numerous occasions. If the Führer's promise of secret weapons had amounted to more than just a promise, Europe and the world might today be of a rather different character.

Although in popular imagining the D in D-Day stands for 'Deliverance', in actual fact D simply stands for day: the day of any military operation is referred to as D-Day, just as the exact hour of its launch is known as H-Hour. That the term should today carry quasi-religious overtones stands as testimony to the unspeakable evil of the regime from which mainland Europe was liberated. The resolve to free Europe took shape almost at the moment the last soldier of the BEF, the British Expeditionary Force, was evacuated from Dunkirk in May 1940. The USA became equally convinced of the merit of liberation after Hitler hastily, and somewhat unwisely, declared war on the US in 1941 following the Japanese sneak attack on Pearl Harbor. Even prior to this incident, however, President Franklin Delano Roosevelt was convinced that a Hitler allowed to consolidate his territorial gains would ultimately come to threaten the security of the US itself.

In the modern era, it is unthinkable that a brutal dictatorship could hold sway over Europe: this, however, is exactly what did happen for four long years after German tanks rushed through France in 1940. The Nazis – their power by now unchallenged in Germany – roared across the continent to the blood-curdling sound of the Stuka dive-bomber, reaching the French coast in just six weeks, a feat the generals of the First World War were unable to achieve in four years.

Operation Sealion

Having lost large numbers of men and materiel in France, the British army was severely understrength and under-equipped and had Hitler decided on a full-scale invasion of the British Isles, there is the likelihood that he may have succeeded. But the Wehrmacht was unprepared for an amphibious assault on this scale, and the High Command was canny enough to recognise this. Disputes between the German army and navy

German troops *in front of the Eiffel Tower, Paris. The speed of the Nazi victory in France took everyone, including Hitler, by surprise.*

August 1940

Pilots of No 610 'County of Chester' Squadron, Royal Auxiliary Air Force resting and talking around their Supermarine Spitfire I fighters on Hawkinge airfield during a lull in the Battle of Britain.

about the logistics of the invasion persuaded Hitler to postpone Operation *Sealion*, as the operation had been codenamed, turning to Göring's Luftwaffe to win control of the skies as a prelude to invasion. The future of the war lay in the hands of the few Royal Air Force pilots – and they prevailed. Operation *Sealion* was shelved indefinitely.

Still clinging to the hope that Britain would sue for peace, Hitler turned his attentions to the Soviet Union, giving British military planners precious time to plot the liberation of Europe. Outside the occupied territories of Europe the conflict raged across many fronts, and the Allies began to have serious discussions about the hazards of invasions.

Valuable lessons were learned with the aborted invasion-style raid on Dieppe in August 1942 although the price was high: the death or capture of some 4,000 Canadian troops.

The Lessons of Dieppe

Firstly, the operation at Dieppe underlined the need for secrecy. At the French port the defending Germans were expecting some action and were well-prepared. Secondly, the Navy's heavy cruisers and battleships would be sorely needed during a large-scale action. At the time the Dieppe raid took place, the Royal Navy was exercising extreme caution in permitting ships into the exposed English Channel and, on this occasion, allowed nothing bigger than a destroyer into the waters to protect the men going ashore. Air supremacy also proved to be crucial, another element missing at Dieppe. Poor communications between beach and operation commanders meant waves of men were sent ashore when they had no hope of survival. This was a further issue that urgently needed addressing as was the lack of meaningful reconnaissance. Many soldiers deposited at Dieppe had no idea where to exit the beach. There was, following Dieppe, a clear need for specialist amphibious craft to protect men emerging from the waters. Perhaps most importantly, the Dieppe fiasco served to highlight the perils of attempting any invasion against established fortifications. As for the Germans, the debacle at Dieppe made them feel impregnable and perhaps contributed to an air of complacency.

There were other, more successful

St Nazaire raids

The Campbelltown *at St Nazaire in the sluice just before she blew up, taking the sluice gate with her.*

Allies united

General Eisenhower greets Free French leader Charles de Gaulle at a meeting of Allied Chiefs in England on the eve of D-Day. Host of the meeting Winston Churchill stands behind them.

landings for the Allies to consider, such as the attack at Vaagso in Norway at the end of 1941, the sabotage of St Nazaire in March 1942 and the so-called Torch landings that propelled additional Allied troops into North Africa in the wake of the success at El Alamein. However, all were on a much smaller scale than D-Day, with far less at stake.

D-Day was a highly ambitious amphibious landing intended to bring a speedy end to the war. Any hitches or reversals would have meant prolonging the conflict, with the additional loss of life that would have involved. In terms of men and materiel, it was a massive undertaking, testing strategy and organisation to the utmost. As Churchill reminded *Overlord* commanders: 'This is an invasion, not the creation of a fortified beachhead.'

Plans were drafted and re-drafted. Whatever his personality clashes with higher officers may have been, the British Field Marshal Sir Bernard Law Montgomery was swift to assess an initial plan as too small. He wanted a much bigger and broader thrust into France in order to prevent the invading forces simply being squeezed back into the sea.

The War of Secrets

The Allies had a fair idea of what awaited them in France. For several years the hierarchy had had access to Germany's military secrets after the Reich's highly complex Enigma code was broken. Germany had been producing Enigma machines since before the war, which, simply put, were 'typewriter' style devices with rotor wheels and plug boards that automatically replaced one letter for another to provide a uniform code. Message recipients also in possession of an Enigma machine simply adjusted their rotors to read off the correctly transposed words. The rotor settings changed on a daily basis. Without specialist knowledge the codes were hopelessly obscure. In fact, the complexity of the encoding system was such that the code-breakers had a one in 150,000,000,000,000,000,000 chance of stumbling across the right answer purely by chance. The German generals sincerely believed the system was impregnable simply because no one would have the time to tackle it. They overlooked some obvious weaknesses: that numbers had to be written in full, that no letter could stand for itself, and that each message began with a weather forecast. They also reckoned without the brilliant mathematicians in Britain who did crack the Enigma code and used it to help Britain win the Battle of the Atlantic by guiding shipping away from known U boat movements.

Still, the Germans had no idea that many of their plans were being shared with the British eavesdroppers working at Bletchley Park, 50 miles north of London. Every effort was made to ensure it stayed that way. It meant that sometimes the military leaders in Britain uncomfortably sat back and let German plans unfold, rather than pre-empt enemy campaigns and jeopardise the access enjoyed by the Allies. It was an advantage they clearly did not want to lose. So when an American task force captured a German U-boat complete with its Enigma code books on 4 June, a mere two days before *Overlord* was scheduled, Commander in Chief of the US Atlantic Fleet, Royal E. Ingersoll, was quick to ensure that not a word of the capture was released until after D-Day was over. Had Germany realised the code was being broken they might have switched systems and closed the window the Allies had on German movements in Normandy just when it was most needed.

The activities of the Allied code-breakers were vital in ensuring that D-Day took place in 1944, rather than, as some analysts believe, 1946, by which time Hitler's secret weapons – the V2 rocket, the so-called 'London gun' and the jet aircraft – may well have been in operation, and the conclusion of the conflict might have been seriously delayed or even altered.

The decision to embark on the D-Day offensive was not entirely straightforward. Britain was already at war on two fronts, in Italy and in Burma. The war in Africa was largely won but had sharply brought into focus the unlikelihood of achieving swift victories over the German army. America was dedicated to squeezing the Japanese out of the Pacific. Indeed, there was considerable domestic pressure in the States – with its sizeable German and Italian populations – to leave the European theatre of war altogether and concentrate on winning the war against the Japanese. But, largely thanks to President Roosevelt, the Americans main-

Enigma machine
Captured German Enigma code machine. Breaking this sophisticated code was a stunning victory for the Allies in the war of intelligence.

Undersea menace
German U-boats in the Atlantic, 1942. At the height of their success the 'wolf-packs' were sinking hundreds of thousands of tons of Allied shipping every week.

tained their 'Germany first' policy, enabling D-Day to go ahead.

At sea the German navy was something of a spent force, although U-boats and E-boats still remained a threat. (Had the U boat packs still been roaming at will the invasion fleet might well have been sunk before it reached French shores.) In the air the Luftwaffe, while still in evidence, was no longer strutting supreme. On land, however, the German Wehrmacht, although stretched and in retreat on the Russian front, was still very much a force to be reckoned with, and would have to be considered carefully in any invasion plan.

Invasion Sites

The next question, then, was the best place to launch the invasion. The obvious site was Calais and the surrounding area, as this was the closest that *Festung Europa* or Fortress Europe lay to Britain. That meant short sea crossings, deeper air cover and tighter supply lines. It was also, however, where the Germans were best prepared for attack. The beaches there were also backed by cliffs, which were impossible to surmount at speed. The next stop down the coast was around Le Havre at the mouth of the River Seine, a major port and likewise heavily defended. Planners toyed with the idea of attacking here but were concerned about the restricted areas available to landing craft.

Further to the west, and further still from the English coast, were the Normandy beaches. Before the war this area was a holiday idyll offering broad, safe beaches, cafes and watersports. Now the beaches were being viewed with a very different eye, as a suitable step off point for countless thousands of Allied troops. Admittedly, there were no ports there to disembark troops and tanks but that was a problem that would be overcome by engineers making portable ports – the sturdy Mulberry harbours – and towing them into position. (No one knows why the floating jetties were named after a tree made famous by a nursery rhyme. One theory is that Churchill recalled with affection the way a Scottish housekeeper pronounced the surname of his ancestors, the Marlboroughs.) The natural advantages of the Normandy beaches, along with lighter fortifications, soon persuaded the military that this was the appropriate gateway for the invasion.

Yet there were other options to discount before the final choice was made. Holland was soon out of the equation for it lay a long way from England and offered no ground cover for invading troops. Norway was more promising though, and Churchill remained intrigued by the possibility of breaching its defences.

To the south lay Portugal and Spain, although any invasion here would have meant using one or two neutral countries as gateways to Europe and their response would not necessarily be favourable. Southern or western France were also suggested and, while both needed elastic supply lines given the distance from England, a co-ordinated attack in the south code named Operation *Anvil* was agreed. Ultimately it was put on ice for six weeks through lack of suitable amphibious craft.

There was great reluctance, especially on Churchill's part, to agree a bombing

The Fox in France
Field Marshal Erwin Rommel (centre) studies a map with other German army officers at Caen, France, during an inspection tour of the coastal defences of the Atlantic Wall.

campaign in northern France to support the invasion force.

It appeared liberating forces were likely to slaughter more French people this way than Germany had during four years of occupation. For Churchill, too, the invasion brought to mind the parallels with the Gallipoli campaign that he had engineered during the First World War and which had ended as a costly fiasco. Indeed, all the key British commanders were mindful of the losses incurred during the First World War and anxious not to replicate the loss of life. A process of elimination left Normandy as the front runner among potential D-Day venues, however.

The next question to be settled was that of who was to take command of the operation. There was clearly a need for close co-operation between British and American commanders. With the US committing the greatest number of men to the operation it fell to the US President to choose a man for the top job, and in January 1944 Roosevelt plumped for General Dwight Eisenhower, a man with some combat experience but whose greatest strength lay in an apparent unflappability and patient diplomacy that would keep the peace between his ambitious subordinates. Beneath him were an array of highly-starred men drawn from both sides of the Atlantic, representing the best military minds of the era with sound experience of operational warfare already behind them. The deputy supreme

commander was Air Chief Marshal Sir Arthur Tedder, a British airman and a veteran of military planning from the Italian campaign.

Among the most senior officers was Montgomery, the victor of El Alamein, a major turning point of the war. Eisenhower once memorably described Montgomery as a 'good man to serve under, a difficult man to serve with and an impossible man to command'.

The brief given to Eisenhower by Washington was simple. 'You will enter the continent of Europe and, in conjunction with the other Allied Nations, undertake operations aimed at the heart of Germany and the destruction of her armed forces.'

Preparations in Britain

The date was fixed for 5 June after planners plotted the lunar cycle. On this day and a few subsequent ones the moon would rise late, thus keeping the first waves of parachutists initially under cover of darkness while offering them the benefit of moonlight after they had landed. The tides would also be low at dawn, giving the invaders a chance to avoid or neutralise beach defences.

Britain itself had also to be prepared. A further 163 airfields were constructed to cater for the massive number of planes needed. Ports were re-organised in order to harbour an unprecedented amount of shipping. No fewer than 170 miles of new railway track had to be laid down to help

Mulberry Harbour

Constructed in England and then towed across the Channel on D-Day, these artificial harbours would provide secure landing places for Allied shipping.

transport supplies. New depots were constructed to accommodate medicines, clothing, food and ammunition.

As the Allies prepared for Operation *Overlord* there was an influx of men and materiel into Britain. By the spring of 1944 some 2,000,000 tons of war materials had been assembled in Britain, including more than 50,000 tanks, armoured cars, jeeps and trucks. One of the major tasks was to mask the scale of the operation taking place from German eyes and this meant disguising the vehicles in woods, on moorland and in warehouses. Then it all had to be filtered through to the relevant ports in time for the start of the invasion.

Joining the Americans and Britons were troops from Canada, Poland, Czechoslovakia, Belgium, Holland, Norway and France, giving an overall total of about two million men. Air squadrons also included Australian, New Zealand, South African and Polish pilots. All had been rehearsed at beaches around the United Kingdom, including Gosport in Hampshire, Studland in Dorset and Westward Ho!, Woolacombe and Slapton Sands in Devon. One exercise at Slapton on 27 April 1944 ended in tragedy when

Screaming Eagles

Eisenhower addresses the men of the US 101st Airborne Division, 'The Screaming Eagles', as they prepare for the D-Day invasion, 5 June 1944.

German E boats slipped through offshore defences and killed 749 American servicemen practising for D-Day. Fears that Germany could have gained access to the *Overlord* plans from the dead bodies of US officers, however, fortunately proved unfounded. Nevertheless, the incident – which claimed more lives than the assault on Utah beach – provided a salutary reminder of the vulnerability of troops in the water; it would also be kept a secret for years afterwards.

Every effort was also made to ensure that *Overlord* remained the nation's best-kept secret. Civilian travel between the UK and Eire was stopped and a belt of coastline ten miles (16 km) deep from the Wash to Land's End was closed to the general public.

An Intelligence Scare

The Allies prided themselves on knowing the identity of German spies in the UK, and keeping them in ignorance. This was an ambitious claim and at least one spy known as Cicero – the code name for Elyeza Bazna – was on the scent of Operation *Overlord*. Bazna was an Albanian working as a valet in the British Embassy in Turkey. If he became party to British secrets it may have been because Allied commanders and diplomats – particularly Churchill – were courting the Turks to come in on the side of the Allies. For his part, Bazna never did manage to discover the date and place of *Overlord*.

British spy chiefs had also been alarmed by some of the clues in the *Daily Telegraph* crossword in the spring of 1944 that revealed remarkable insights into the secret operations to re-take Europe. Clues such as: 'But some big-wig like this has stolen some of it at times' with the answer 'Overlord', and 'The bush is a centre of nursery revolutions', with the answer 'mulberry' caused alarm amongst the British intelligence community, as did two further clues that appeared during May with answers that were also code names for the beaches being used for the invasion.

The crossword compiler, Leonard Dawe, a 54-year-old science teacher from Leatherhead in Surrey, was duly visited by agents of MI5, the branch of British Intelligence responsible for security at home, who had more than a few questions to put to the unfortunate Dawe: in a later BBC interview Dawe admitted: 'They turned me inside out.'

Dawe himself put the entire incident down to a bizarre coincidence. In fact, a likely explanation for this supposed security breach emerged much later. According to Ronald French, one of Dawe's pupils at Strand School, South London, the teacher would let boys insert words into his puzzle grids while he thought up clues to match them. By 1944 the entire school had been evacuated to Effingham, Surrey, and was next door to a huge camp of American and Canadian soldiers. These men used the codewords openly – though they didn't know their significance. Ronald French, who spent his every spare moment in their company, simply passed the words on to his headmaster.

'Everyone knew the outline invasion plan and they knew the various codewords,' he recalled later. 'Omaha and Utah were the beaches they were going to. They knew the names but not the locations. We all knew the operation was called Overlord.

'I was obviously not a German spy.

Hundreds of kids must have known what I knew.'

There were anyway more spectacularly awful leaks from loyal members of staff to contend with, not least an American general and a British colonel who let slip vital information, no doubt to improve their standing among their peers. Worse still, a teletype operator practising during the night of 4 June dispatched the message that the Allied landing had started. The result was panic among the Allied commanders – and crucially confusion among those in Germany who presumed it was some kind of hoax.

In retrospect it seems astonishing that the Germans were not thoroughly acquainted with the British plans. Those in the Reich charged with reconaissance might have been taken in by the tent city that sprang up in Kent, complete with tanks and ships in the relevant ports. There was even smoke rising from the tents each day to indicate large scale cooking and hectic radio activity to simulate the approach of a major operation. It was impossible to distinguish from the air that the tents were empty, the tanks were made of rubber and the ships were plywood. This was Operation *Fortitude* and it was all a ruse to make German commanders believe that an invasion force, the mythical First US Army Group (FUSAG) under General George S Patton, was bound for Calais. This ensured that German commanders, including Hitler himself, kept one eye on the region around Calais. It was so successful that even after the Normandy landings were underway, Hilter remained convinced that they were a diversion. The main force, he believed, would land at Calais. On 1 June German eavesdroppers noted 'a personal message' on a BBC news bulletin that consisted of the first verse of 'Chanson d'Automne' by the 19th century French poet Paul Verlaine. It went: 'Les sanglots long, des violons de l'automne', meaning 'The long sighing of the violins of autumn'. They had already been forewarned that this was an initial alert to the French resistance about a forthcoming invasion. (Listening to the BBC was a capital offence in the Reich but was nonetheless a widespread practice.) The broadcasting of the second verse was a signal that the invasion was imminent.

Although one warning was subsequently issued to the German Fifteenth Army, other significant commanders and army groups were not told. One of the Field Marshals apparently left in the dark was Rommel, who returned to Germany on 4 June on the pretext of attending a meeting – in fact, he wanted to be with his wife on her birthday. If he knew about the first message and its significance he must have discounted it. He certainly wasn't at his post when the second half of the message was broadcast: 'Blessent mon coeur d'une langeueur monotone', or 'Wound my heart with a monotonous languor.' It was read out by a BBC presenter on the evening of 5 June as parachutists were already blacked up and strapped up, as convoys were cutting a swathe through the Channel. German radio operators pounced upon the long-awaited sign. Yet still only the Fifteenth Army was put on alert as army commanders pondered the likelihood of British and Americans announcing an impending invasion through the BBC.

Purely by coincidence, German commanders had scheduled a *Kriegsspiel* or war game for 6 June at Rennes in Brittany,

a map exercise to prepare them for an invasion beginning with paratrooper landings and followed with beach landings in Normandy. Although commanders were instructed not to leave their posts until 6 June, many were already en route when the real invasion began.

The Atlantic Wall

In some ways the Nazis were prepared for the Allied invasion. The OKW – *Oberkommando Wehrmacht*, the German High Command – had in early 1942 ordered the construction of the Atlantic Wall, a long, snaking line of concrete fortifications and emplacements stretching from Norway to Spain. It was a grandiose scheme that had been much talked about in high level conferences but actually did not amount to very much, as Field Marshal Erwin Rommel discovered on being transferred to France from North Africa. Many of the gun emplacements were half finished, fewer than half of the required mines had been laid, and the troops manning the defences had grown complacent and lazy.

During the early months of 1944 Rommel began mounting an energetic attempt to bring defences up to scratch. Upon his orders some four million mines were laid along the Channel coast before

Outgunned
American engineers inspect a captured German gun emplacement along the cliffs of Normandy. The emplacement was part of Hitler's 'Atlantic Wall' defensive line.

the arrival of the Allies – a fraction of the number he planned ultimately. When mines proved hard to come by Rommel insisted that other armaments were modified so that explosive fields could be completed, and also supervised the construction of assorted beach defences designed to thwart access for tanks. The Germans used forced French labour to complete these tasks.

In doing so they inadvertently gave away vital secrets. A painter named Rene Duchez sneaked out a blueprint of the Atlantic Wall defences from Rommel's headquarters in Caen. Realising a copy of the plans was missing, the Germans sum-

Montgomery of Alamein

Field Marshal Bernard Montgomery, pictured here in front of a Grant tank. General Eisenhower described Montgomery: 'a good man to serve under, a difficult man to work with and an impossible man to command'.

marily shot an innocent electrician believing him to be the spy. Duchez – who was never left unaccompanied in the building but still accomplished the theft – sent the documents on the intelligence network to London. Artillerymen and engineers were given the information as they planned the assault of the Atlantic defences.

In some ways the planning of D-Day is a much longer and more intricate story than D-Day itself. It was years in the making, the product of some of the finest military and political brains of the day. It was debated at length until its authors sensed some kind of perfection. There were personality clashes – most notably between Montgomery and almost every American involved at every level – and logistical problems on an immense scale. Nonetheless, when it came together it was a remarkable exercise in co-operation among numerous nations who largely put national interest further down the agenda for the sake of victory against Hitler's Nazis. Part of its success was down to the personal chemistry between the two most significant players, Sir Winston Churchill and President Roosevelt. Both recognised the importance of maintaining a united front between themselves and the third significant Allied leader, Soviet premier Josef Stalin.

A Second Front

There was increasing pressure from Stalin who felt – perhaps with some justification – that his soldiers were bearing the brunt of the campaign against Germany, and pressed the Western Allies to open up a second front with a cross-Channel invasion. The fighting on the Eastern Front was of a different order entirely to that which took place in North Africa: in the savage clashes between German and Russian troops no quarter was given and none was expected.

Among Stalin's private concerns was that Churchill and Roosevelt would manipulate a prolonged war of attrition between the German and Red Army forces to weaken Russia in readiness for a post-war collapse of Communism. While both democratic leaders made little secret of their distaste for Communism, there is no evidence that this secret agenda ever existed.

However, the intensity of the war in the east would be both a blessing and a curse for the Allies. The majority of Germany's battle-ready troops were embroiled in the conflict, leaving the western borders of the Reich as a defensive backwater inhabited by the old, the young and those recuperating from action in the east. On the other hand, when relatively inexperienced American troops landed on Omaha beach, they discovered battle-hardened veterans from the Eastern front waiting for them, ready to fight with the fervour they knew against the Red Army. The potential horrors were obvious, at least to Marshal Henri Petain, the puppet ruler of Vichy France, a state set up after the German invasion of France, nominally with its own government but in reality a satellite state of the Reich. On the day of the invasion he broadcast from Paris warning French people: 'The trend of the battle may lead the German army to take special measures in the battle areas. Accept this necessity.'

The Reich in Retreat

Militarily, the Reich was feeling the pinch by 1944. The Red Army had made considerable gains on the Eastern Front and were pressing hard on Germany's frontiers. The defeat inflicted by the Russians on the Germans at Stalingrad in 1943 had left the Wehrmacht and its high command reeling. There had been some recovery time by now, however, and the German forces were braced for an attack by the Allies even if they were unsure where it would take place. What they could not tolerate was a long war of attrition. The Reich's supplies were perpetually dwindling and it was proving impossible to make up the shortfall, mostly due to Allied aerial bombardment.

For his part Hitler remained certain of eventual victory. The setbacks that blighted his daily conferences were, he was convinced, caused by bungling generals in the Wehrmacht. His blistering invective against those highly decorated and professional men was awesomely vindictive.

On 4 June the weather forecast was

The Eastern Front, 1944
After three years of bitter fighting against the German army on his home soil, Stalin was eager for the Western Allies to open up the Second Front in Normandy.

unseasonably bleak and, reluctantly, Eisenhower took a decision to postpone the invasion for 24 hours. Shipping convoys that had already sailed so as to be in position on 5 June were turned around just before they came into enemy sights. The crew of midget submarines sent to a particularly featureless bit of the Normandy coast as markers had to sit on the seabed in cramped, stuffy conditions until conditions were ripe. Ships that had already been prepared now had to be refuelled and re-organised. Queasy troops were penned into the ships as commanders waited nervously for the gales to subside. Just how long could men primed for battle and at the pinnacle of readiness be kept in uncomfortable isolation?

The decision lay with one man. Before he came to his final decision Dwight Eisenhower went for a largely silent walk with NBC correspondent Merrill Mueller. Afterwards, Mueller commented that Eisenhower was 'bowed down with worry . . . as though each of the four stars on either shoulder weighed a ton.'

Meteorologists were convinced that the poor weather would give way to a clear

Allied Armada

A fleet of Allied landing ships makes its way towards the coast of Normandy. The ships are towing barrage balloons, to prevent enemy air attacks.

spell. However, that was forecast to last for just 24 hours before inclement conditions closed in again. If the delay was to be just for 24 hours then a final decision would be needed promptly in order that the chain of events could once again begin. If it was to be postponed indefinitely then it would be a full two weeks before it could be attempted again. Eisenhower surveyed the options carefully before deciding the invasion would take place for sure on 6 June.

Following his decision he dispatched a message to the troops.

'You are about to embark upon the Great Crusade, toward which we have striven these many months. The eyes of the world are upon you. The hopes and prayers of liberty-loving people everywhere march with you. In company with our brave Allies and brothers-in-arms on other Fronts you will bring about the destruction of the German war machine, the elimination of Nazi tyranny over the oppressed peoples of Europe and security for ourselves in a free world.'

On 5 June 1944 Operation *Neptune* – the marine side of the D-Day – swung fully into action. Thousands of vessels set sail from Britain, including 1,200 fighting ships, 4,126 landing craft and 804 transport ships. Britain provided most of the shipping, although 17 per cent came from the US, including 30 destroyers, while ships were also provided by Canada, Holland, Norway, France and Greece. For a while the seas off the Isle of Wight were dubbed 'Piccadilly Circus' as each craft found its earmarked spot in the convoy lanes so all lay in the correct running order. To some observers it seemed you could have walked across the Channel without getting your feet wet. There would be space enough on the water for 1,400 small landing craft carried for now in heavy transports as well as hospital ships, tugs, tankers and merchant ships towing barrage balloons. Among the vessels were ten LB (K)s – landing barges (kitchen) – which were floating galleys to provide sailors from small craft and soldiers with a hot meal. Between them they could cater for up to 7,000 men a day as well as producing 1,000 pounds of bread. In the skies above there were some 10,000 military aircraft.

In overall charge was Admiral Sir Bertram Ramsay who had distinguished himself during the evacuation of Dunkirk. In turn he was reliant on the navigation skills of naval officers and pilots, who themselves depended on the accuracy of the information gathered by beach reconnaissance parties who had worked under cover of darkness at great personal risk in the months previously. The German naval response to this build-up was negligible. Four German torpedo boats sank a Norwegian destroyer before hightailing it out of the area. Two US destroyers, the *Corry* and the *Meredith*, struck mines and sank on D-Day along with some smaller craft. German shore batteries achieved just one significant strike, against a British LCI.

On board the Allied ships there were 132,000 young men destined for the beaches. They waited with trepidation, unsure precisely what lay ahead. Some were veterans of other invasion forces while others were rookies, seeing this kind of action for the first time. They talked, prayed, wrote letters home and slept when they could. The conviction among most of the men was that they would die at the hands of the German defenders. They had taken a noble path, to lay down their lives for their country for the common good. But it should not be forgotten that most of these extreme risk-takers – those landing at H-hour on D-Day – were doing so reluctantly.

The vast majority of men were repeatedly seasick. The weight of expectation was huge but even that was put in the shade by the effects of nausea. Corporal Hughie Rocks of the Queen's Own Rifles of Canada spoke for many confined in boats off Normandy beaches in the early hours of 6 June when he said: 'I don't care if there are 50 million Germans on the beach; just let me off this goddamn boat!'

Spare a thought too for the average German soldier on coastal patrol on 6 June, expecting this day to be much like any other. As dawn rose upon the Channel an awesome sight would have been revealed. The blue waters were dark with the immense steel-hulled armada and the skies were shadowy with successive volleys of aircraft whose combined engine noise made everything vibrate. The impulse for flight above fight must have been great.

The Airborne Assault

This was the scene arrayed before the German coastal patrols. They did not know that some 23,500 British and American troops had already been dropped inland. As they swung to earth the men of the airborne divisions were mindful of the threat posed by enemy fire. In fact, there was little organised resistance on the ground, the greatest danger coming from the swamps around the rivers Douve and Merderet and the Dives valley flooded by Rommel in preparation for the invasion. An unknown number drowned as they were pinned to river beds by their equipment and still more were killed in glider crashes. Numerous parachutists became disorientated and simply got lost. However, the survivors who managed to make their rendezvous points or reorganise with those that did set about sabotaging German communication links and securing vital bridges. American parachutists had a shaky start to their campaign in one venue. Some 20 parachutists came down in a village square, to be instantly killed or taken prisoner by bemused resident Germans. One man's chute became tangled with the church steeple. He dangled there for more than two hours, pretending to be dead, before the Germans caught on and captured him. Nevertheless, men from the 82nd Airborne Division liberated St Mere Eglise, the first village to be freed from German occupation, at dawn.

Pegasus Bridge

Men of the British 6th Airborne Division had one specific task, to capture two bridges that crossed the Caen Canal and the River Orne at Benouville. The force that held this bridge controlled the movement of forces from the Normandy beaches to the east, specifically the Pas de Calais. Had it been in German hands it would surely have been freely used by the divisions assigned to defend the more northerly coast against invasion after it became clear the action had already begun. It has since been named Pegasus Bridge, for the division's winged horse insignia.

It was on Pegasus Bridge that the first German victim of Allied land-based troops was claimed. It was a young sentry,

Pegasus Bridge

This crucial bridge over the River Orne was captured in the early hours of D-Day by the British 6th Airborne Division, after whose winged horse emblem the bridge is now named.

The Longest Day

On the set of the film of the same name are the heroes who captured the bridge, and the actors who played them: (l to r) Peter Lawford, Lord Lovat, Richard Todd, Major John Howard.

cut down as he fired a flare to alert fellow soldiers about the presence of enemy paratroopers. Moments later the first British casualty was felled by German machine gunners. It took barely eight seconds for Lieutenant Herbert Denham Brotheridge to enter history as the first Allied soldier to die on D-Day.

Brotheridge had been a Weights and Measures inspector at Smethwick Council before volunteering for the Army in 1937. Three years later he married Maggie, and their first and only child, Margaret, was born on 25 June 1944, 19 days after Brotheridge's death.

Had Lieutenant Brotheridge survived, his dream would have been to play professional football: before the war he had been on Aston Villa's books as a reserve.

He had been hand picked to lead one of six 30-man companies in action that night by Major John Howard. Brotheridge's glider crash-landed into the barbed wire defences at about 2am on 6 June and his men were first on to the bridge.

The story of Lieutenant Brotheridge and the audacious assault by six glider-borne platoons of the 2nd Battalion the Oxfordshire and Bucks Light Infantry (since amalgamated into the Royal Greenjackets) ranks among the Second World War's greatest adventures.

It was later dramatised in the film *The Longest Day*, starring Richard Burton, Sean Connery, and Robert Mitchum.

Brotheridge's daughter Margaret discovered the truth about her heroic father years later. 'The bullets hit him in the neck, literally within seconds. They eventually managed to get him to Madame Gondrée's cafe at the far end and she was with him when he died a short time later.'

Before the 50th anniversary of D-Day Margaret made a low-key visit to the cafe – the first house in Nazi-occupied Europe to be liberated. With only limited French, she could offer no explanation other than hand her passport to Madame Gondrée.

'She stared at me for a few seconds,' Margaret recalled. 'Then she shoved all her customers out, closed the door and sat holding my hand in silence.

'After that she produced a huge meal, which we couldn't eat, gathered flowers from all the tables and tied them with French ribbon. Then she pointed us to my father's grave.

'She had done her best to make him comfortable as he died. We couldn't talk about it but then nothing really needed to be said.'

Members of Madame Gondrée's family had risked their lives prior to D-Day to provide intelligence about the bridge and its defences.

Another key source about her father's

Mme Arlette Gondrée

Owner of the Cafe Gondrée at Pegasus Bridge, her family was the first in France to be liberated by Allied forces in the early hours of 6 June, 1944.

exploits has been Colonel David Wood MBE, the last surviving officer of the Pegasus operation.

He and Brotheridge were both lieutenants in command of platoons and knew each other well. They spent weeks training for the attack using bridges on the Exeter Canal and the River Exe, Exeter.

Colonel Wood, 81, who was himself wounded at Pegasus, recalls Lieutenant Brotheridge as a superb soldier.

'He was a corporal in the Army when Major Howard spotted him and put him up for a commission. 'That was extremely unusual. It wasn't easy for men from the ranks to become officers.'He commanded enormous respect from his platoon. His authority was unquestioned yet he could go down to the barracks and smoke with the men, tell jokes and talk football. He was exceptionally well-liked which was why his death affected people so deeply.

'There is no doubt in my mind that,

A Fallen Hero

Gravestone of Lieutenant Herbert Brotheridge, the first Allied soldier to be killed in the liberation of France. The Gondree family's plaque in his memory is to the left.

had he survived, he would have won the Military Cross. Sadly, he didn't live long enough.'

Colonel Wood has since revealed how airborne troops nearly didn't get off the ground. After three days round-the-clock practice at two swing bridges on the River Exe and the Exeter Canal in Exeter, the men were paid a day early and hit the city's pubs with a vengeance as they awaited invasion orders.

Many were arrested and detained by police – threatening to severely weaken the task force before it had even left England.

Colonel Wood said: 'The men were absolutely sick of the sight of those practice bridges. Night and day they'd been put through a seemingly endless and complicated series of rehearsals, attacking both bridges from different directions using a variety of permutations.

'Finally, they found themselves let loose on Exeter. There was pub crawling, some drank too much and damage was done to more than one window.

'It took a personal approach by our company commander, a former policeman, and an understanding senior police officer – himself a First World War veteran – to get everyone back to camp without facing charges.

'The people of Exeter were really very good about it.'

Other airborne troops were able to capitalise on the surprise element of the attack, wiping out small German posts.

Then they hunkered down, waiting to support the influx of Allied troops from the beach. Before those troops could land the bombers were to pound the beaches to make their passage safer. This was the announcement of the impending invasion for most of the local French people. Many were braced for Allied action although most probably assumed it would be further up the coast rather than in their vicinity. While different cells of the resistance had been assigned tasks of assassination and sabotage only a few resistance workers knew the extent of the Allied plan.

Even German commanders were unsure about whether or not D-Day had begun. The bad weather had lulled many into thinking the invasion was not imminent. It was likely to happen, they believed, when the weather was set fair. In addition, air attacks around Calais and the apparent activity of Allied troops across the Channel in Kent had made it difficult to determine the destination of the Allied forces until they were actually in sight. A majority of German radar stations in Normandy had been knocked out by Allied aircraft. The remainder showed that a fake armada setting sail from Dover looked far more of a threat than the real one off the Normandy beaches. Around Le Havre Allied aircraft dropped WINDOW, a kind of foil that showed up on radar screen as ships, and they helped to block radio traffic. In addition, dummy parachutists as well as real ones were dropped to help fudge German thinking.

Order of Battle, D-Day 6 June 1944

Allied Divisions

21st Army Group

Second (British) Army

79th Armoured Division

6th Airborne Divsion

49th (West Riding) Division

50th (Northumbrian) Division

51st (Highland) Division

3rd Canadian Division

12th US Army Group

First and Third US Armies

82nd Airborne Division

101st Airborne Division

1st Infantry Division

4th Infantry Division

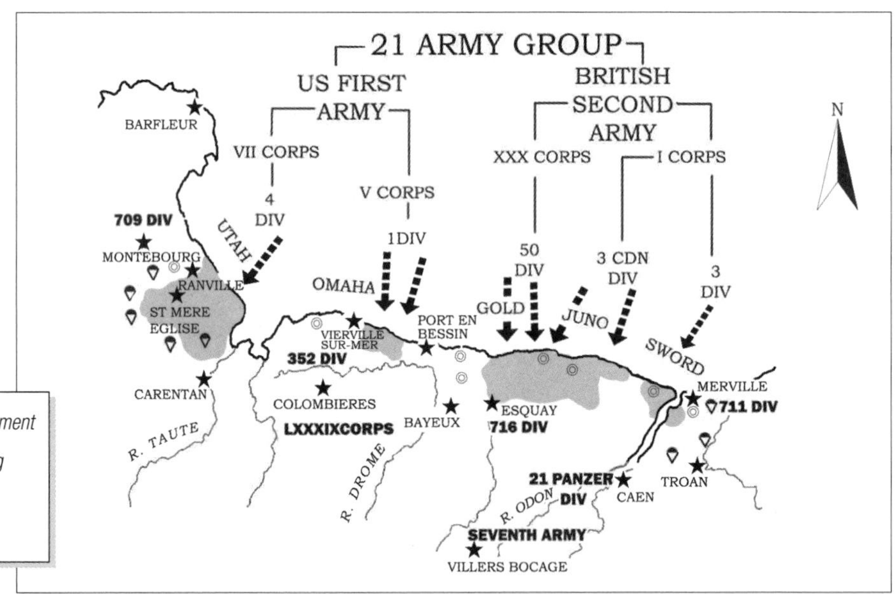

German gun emplacement

Allied airborne landing

Allied gains midnight 6th june

German Divisions

Seventh Army

77th Infantry Division

91st Infantry Division

243rd Infantry Division

265th Infantry Division

266th Infantry Division

275th Infantry Division

343rd Infantry Division

352nd Infantry Division

353rd Infantry Division

709th Infantry Division

716th Infantry Division

2nd Parachute Division

3rd Parachute Division

5th Parachute Division

Airborne Assault

Hundreds of parachutes fall towards the fields of Normandy as the airborne part of Operation Overlord gets underway.

At The Ready

US soldier takes up position in front of a Waco glider, Normandy.

CHAPTER TWO

The Normandy Landings

'This operation will be the primary United States–British ground and air effort against the Axis in Europe'

Joint Chiefs of Staff report,
First Quebec Conference, August 1943

Ten Allied divisions, including the three airborne, were pitched into *Overlord*, along with naval support. Awaiting them in Normandy – although not all on the beaches – were 25 static coastal divisions, 16 infantry and parachute divisions, ten armoured and mechanical divisions and seven reserve divisions.

As a grey dawn light ushered in D-Day the infantrymen were poised to surge up the Normandy beaches in a crucial first step to the liberation of France. American forces of the 1st and 4th Infantry Divisions were heading for beaches code-named 'Utah' and 'Omaha' while the British 49th (West Riding), 50th (Northumbrian) and 51st (Highland) Infantry Divisions, together with the Canadian 3rd Division and supported by 79th Armoured Division were heading for 'Juno', 'Sword' and 'Gold' beaches. The five beaches were sited along a 55-mile stretch of coast and each one was broad and divided into sections. The bombs of the Allied air forces were frequently wide of their targets so all the beaches had some defences remaining in position. While some troops landed without difficulty others in a neighbouring zone on the same beach came under fire. Those divisions comprising the first wave of men up the beaches suffered the most losses. The air was acrid with smoke palls.

Concerned about the threat from German gun emplacements, the British commanders held back beach landings so that navy guns and military aircraft could bomb the beaches more comprehensively. This had a knock-on effect throughout the day, occasionally depriving men of covering fire when it was most needed.

The British invasion forces also had the benefit of 'Hobart's Funnies' – various specialised variations of tanks designed by Major General Percy Hobart to assist vulnerable infantrymen up the beach. These included the Crab, a Sherman tank fitted with an anti-mine flail device, the AVRE (Assault Vehicle Royal Engineers), a bridge-laying tank, and the Duplex-Drive, the so-called 'swimming tank', designed to reach the beaches before the infantry and provide cover.

The British Beaches

On Gold the invaders met organised resistance from the Germans and a solid section of the Atlantic Wall. There were also more underwater obstacles here than at other beaches, and as the day progressed, the troops on Gold, as on all the

Hit the Beaches

US infantry disembark their landing craft and make their way toward Omaha beach, under overwhelming enemy fire.

other beaches, were pushed up the sands by the swollen waters of a flood tide, leaving frustrated sappers unable to complete the task of clearing beach obstacles. Many died on the sands as the beach was swept with fire. But the German bullets were insufficient to halt the steady stream of men each charged with a task on the beach or beyond to help secure a safe passage for those following. Pill boxes and gun emplacements were eventually knocked out by aircraft or naval guns. George Laity, a gunner with the 2nd Devons later recalled:

'The barrage, the noise, the infantry, the little LCAs . . . it was all confusion and bewilderment. German 88s started pounding the beach. My company was pinned down and it seemed endless.'

By the afternoon, however, the defenders had been pushed back. Soldiers who had a smoother passage on to the beach had to fight in the dunes, swamps and countryside nearby.

Three VCs

Sergeant-Major Stan Hollis of the Green Howards Regiment, who won the Victoria Cross on D-Day, pictured at Buckingham Palace to receive his medal. With him are Major Sidney of the Grenadier Guards (l) and Brigadier Campbell of the Argyll and Sutherland Highlanders.

One man who went into action on Gold beach was later given the Victoria Cross for his actions. Company Sergeant-Major Stan Hollis of the Green Howards single-handedly cleared a pill box and a trench and also staged a distraction to save two other men from being killed by drawing enemy fire. His official citation reads:

'Wherever fighting was heaviest CSM Hollis appeared, and in the course of a magnificent day's work he displayed the utmost gallantry, and on two separate occasions his courage and initiative prevented the enemy from holding up the advance at critical stages. It was largely through his heroism and resource that the Company's objectives were gained and casualties were not heavier and by his own bravery he saved the lives of many of his men.'

By the end of the day the casualties on Gold amounted to about 1,000.

Of the 24,000 who attacked Juno beach 15,000 were Canadians while 9,000 were British. In common with other beaches the men of the first wave were thwarted by capsizing craft and enemy guns. The initial pounding by bombers had largely failed in its objective of making the thoroughfare safer. The war diary of the Royal Winnipeg Rifles offers evidence once again that the pounding by aircraft and navy big ships failed to significantly dent defences.

It read: '09.00 hrs. The bombardment having failed to kill a single German or silence one weapon, (army companies) had to storm their positions "cold" and did so without hesitation.'

The war diary of the Queen's Own Rifles of Canada records that at 09 40 hrs

'. . . it is noted that a café just 100 yards off the beach is opened up and selling wine to all and sundry'.

Sword beach was also reduced to chaos although once again men quickly made it to the exits. German defenders, at first surprised by the onslaught, soon recovered and mounted a stiff resistance.

Glaswegian George Ross was a sergeant major in one of the beach groups at Sword aiming to establish a safe route for tanks:

'I honestly cannot say I was nervous. I was anxious but I had been warned about what to expect during six months of lectures beforehand.

'There were bodies in the water of both British and Germans. One of the officers

To the Beaches

American DUKWs – two-and-a-half ton trucks fitted with flotation tanks and propellors – make their way towards Omaha beach.

told us afterwards how, when he was walking up the beach, he felt he was walking on cushions. It was bodies of dead soldiers he was walking on.'

It was at Sword beach that Lord Lovat and his hand-picked Commandos – including German anti-fascists – disembarked with piper Bill Millin. Lovat walked through the water with the aid of a walking stick with his head held high. He had recruited Millin in direct contravention of War Office regulations. The aim was to boost morale – although the piper also served to draw enemy fire, to the consternation of soldiers nearby.

Afterwards Millin said: 'Wounded men were shocked to see me. They had wanted to see a doctor. Instead they saw me in my kilt, playing the bagpipes. It was horrifying as I felt so helpless.' He witnessed a British Crab flail tank drive straight over wounded Allied soldiers but had little time to dwell on the tragedy. He was soon back in action playing *Road to the Isles* up and down the beach.

The American Beaches

At Utah the landings were a textbook exercise. This was mainly because the airborne troops had knocked out German resistance before it could begin firing in anger. Out of 23,000 men landed on Utah beach on 6 June there were only 197 dead and wounded.

It was a different story on neighbouring Omaha beach where low cloud prevented the bombers from mounting successful raids prior to the landings. At first battleship bombardments also fell short, leaving the German guns largely unscathed. However, when the difficulties facing the beached troops became starkly apparent, the skippers of the supporting destroyers risked everything by bringing their vessels close to shore to provide as much cover as possible.

The defenders at Omaha were the battle-hardened men of the 352nd division who, unknown to the Allies, had moved into position as recently as May having returned from the eastern front. There

was also a range of man-made defences installed to complement the natural obstacles of cliffs and shingle.

In the confusion officers signalled the release of amphibious tanks far too early, dispatching many to the bottom of the sea with their crews on board.

The low tide meant soldiers had a distance of several hundred yards to cover before achieving the shelter of high ground. That included zones covered with beach defences. Wave upon wave of men disembarked, stepping over the bodies of comrades, to face slaughter themselves. A number fell victim to machine-gun fire as the doors of the landing craft opened before setting foot on enemy-held territory, tumbling into blood-stained waves.

Advance

Soldiers of the 3rd Canadian Division ready themselves for the attack at Colombelle, Normandy.

Progress was painfully slow among men hampered by heavy equipment, wet clothes and, of course, enemy fire. Snipers picked off those who made it on to the sands finding the steel hedgehogs inadequate shelter from the hail of bullets raining down.

Soon a rising tide drowned the wounded who lay in its path and pushed other men further into the line of fire as the day unfolded. Supporting troops and machinery were later kept at bay by intact beach defences, units were split, radio communications non existent, escape routes cluttered by wreckage. The scramble continued for hours until an advance on the beach heights was begun about noon. Only during the afternoon did the American troops on Omaha succeed in silencing the German guns. Landing craft that brought the ill-fated fighting men to the beach were swiftly put on stand by to carry out an evacuation although ultimately this did not prove necessary.

William Ryan, an 18 year old in the US 16th Infantry Regiment, was injured landing in the first wave at Omaha.

'I was blown over the side (of an LCVP) and knocked unconscious. I was told later that two of the men in the boat with me dragged me through the water and propped me up against an embankment. Otherwise I would have drowned.

'At first there were five or six wounded with me. Then there were hundreds. I lay on the beach in that same position from about 8 am until 10 pm when they evacuated us. I had concussion in addition to shell fragments in my head, shoulder and leg. All this time I was going in and out of consciousness, looking down on Omaha beach. It was just a mad house. Troops were pinned down by the gun emplacements. Eventually a US Navy destroyer came in as close to the beach as possible without running aground and started firing at all the German emplacements. In a little while two or three other destroyers started shelling as well. In my opinion that is what saved Omaha beach from defeat.

'I heard afterwards the skipper on the ship was ordered to go back to a safe position. Apparently he said he wasn't leaving while US soldiers were pinned down on the beach. He could have been court martialled for what he did. But he should have got a medal.'

In fact naval bombardment proved ineffective against the most entrenched German guns, although it did succeed in knocking out lesser emplacements.

Harry Mannington was a British crewman on a landing craft who got pitched into the beach battle at Omaha when the beachmaster, responsible for keeping traffic moving, was short of men. He went

On the Beach

The scene on the British beach as further waves of troops are disembarked from LCIs – Landing Craft Infantry – to take their places in the front line.

Bloody Omaha

The struggle for Omaha beach, as seen through the eyes of Dwight Shepler, Official US Navy Combat Artist.

ashore with no gun and no training. 'You were on your own. My only thought was to survive. There were terrible sights – a man with no arms and all that. I could hear people screaming and calling out for their mothers. But if you started worrying about them you'd soon be joining them. I thought; how mad it is that people can do this to each other.'

The final death toll on Omaha remains unclear, but it is thought that some 2,500 men died before D-Day was over. Perhaps three times that number were wounded and three sets of brothers were among those killed. The US V Corps sustained 2,000 casualties alone. Thereafter it was known as 'Bloody Omaha'.

By the close of D-Day – quickly dubbed 'the longest day' – about 155,000 Allied troops were ashore. Rookie soldiers had become veterans within the space of just 24 hours. They learned to step over the bodies of fallen comrades without contemplating the tragedy. They also instinctively worked to save the lives of fellow soldiers wherever possible. Some of their places aboard the landing craft heading back for England were taken by German prisoners of war. In one sense D-Day was a failure, as few if any of the targets set by the military planners had been achieved. Planners had also inaccurately assessed the affect of roaring currents in the sea that threw many men and craft off course. And yet despite the lack of achievement here, the lack of depth in the invasion and the alarming death toll (which was actually far less than some had feared) it was a resounding success. Careful planning had paid dividends and, in contrast to Dunkirk, Allied aircraft had mastery of the skies, leaving the Luftwaffe inert. Germany's hold on occupied Europe had been broken. The fingers of the Reich's clenched fist were forced open a little and the grip was loosened.

On the evening of 6 June Winston Churchill addressed the House of Commons:

'During the night and the early hours of this morning the first of a series of landings in force upon the European Continent has taken place. In this case the liberating assault fell on France. . . .

'So far the Commanders who are engaged report that everything is proceeding according to plan. And what a plan! This vast operation is undoubtedly the most complicated and difficult that has ever taken place . . .

'There are already hopes that actual tactical surprise has been attained, and we hope to furnish the enemy with a succession of surprises during the course of the fighting. The battle that has now begun will grow constantly in scale and in intensity for many weeks to come and I shall not attempt to speculate upon its course.'

For his part, Hitler was more than willing to speculate on the coming course of the war, telling his senior generals that they should celebrate the Allied landings, as now at last they were within reach of the Wehrmacht, and could be destroyed. Once again, Hitler's optimism would prove to be unfounded.

A Richer Dust

A moment of quiet reflection on the 60th anniversary of D-Day for a veteran of the Normandy landings

CHAPTER THREE

Into the Bocage

'You know where you are going. We are going to hold there till hell freezes over or we are relieved, whichever comes first'

Lieutenant Colonel William Yarborough, US Army

British roads that had rumbled with military traffic in the days and weeks leading up to D-Day were now empty. Pubs and clubs that had echoed to the whoops and laughter of soldiers from Britain and across the Atlantic lay deserted as the men and machines that had become a familiar element of daily life all vanished at a stroke. Residents of southern British villages and towns were left to wonder about the fate of men they had grown to know well.

Something similar to the sense of uneasy tranquility that pervaded southern Britain was being felt in northern France. However, the roads of France were by contrast suddenly awash with traffic as German commanders belatedly realised the invasion had begun. Units that had been held back from the Normandy coast were now sent there at speed to stem the flow of Allied troops. A delay in the chain of command occurred as members of staff were too fearful to wake Hitler from his sleep to inquire about troop movements. On being belatedly informed about the invasion he told those around him to relish the inevitable victory.

Among those on the road was Erwin Rommel, frantically driving from a short break in Germany back to his post. 'If I was commanding the Allied forces right now, I could win the war in fourteen days,' he confided to a colleague.

Perhaps, but the taking of Normandy proved no easy task. It was three weeks after D-Day that US troops liberated the peninsular port of Cherbourg, and it was not until 18 July that British and Canadian troops captured the well-fortified city of Caen, just 7.5 miles (12 km) from the coast and scheduled to fall on the first day of the campaign to the men who landed at 'Sword'. In the immediate aftermath of D-Day soldiers in France and their families at home revived that old World War One adage: 'it will all be over by Christmas'. In fact Christmas 1944 would be one of the coldest, bloodiest and altogether grimmest of the conflict.

The Allies could not seem to put a steady foot on the accelerator through Normandy. The initial reasons for some fatal stalls were numerous. Some men dug in when they should have advanced. Poor intelligence regarding the whereabouts of German soldiers meant that weary soldiers were pitched into battles swiftly and unexpectedly – and failed to win them. A bold counterattack by the 21st Panzer division halted the drive on Caen. Germans everywhere in Normandy fought with

considerably more resolve than was generally expected. There was a mammoth amount of chaos, with men split from their units and severed from the command chain. Casualties continued to mount, even after the spectre of D-Day, and morale dipped as tense periods of waiting, watching and foot-slogging became the norm. Some French villages were liberated then lost again in a matter of hours.

Frequently the underlying cause of the Allied lack of success lay in questionable tactical approaches taken by the British commander Montgomery and the American General Omar Bradley. Some of those decisions were brought about by a startling lack of intelligence about the nature of the Normandy countryside. The area was covered with ancient hedgerows between six and twenty feet in height growing atop earth banks, a system known by the French word *bocage*. Although the barriers were man-made they had existed since Roman times and were well entrenched.

Back at *Overlord* HQ – where the emphasis had focused very much on a successful D-Day operation – the existence of the *bocage* had been noted but no firm theories had evolved about how to deal with it. Planners could not work out

A Hasty Farewell

Secrecy was a vital part of Operation Overlord; as such, even the men who would be undertaking the operation were kept in the dark until the last possible moment.

whether the hedges would help or hinder progressing Allied troops. Despite numerous mock assaults on British beaches, there had been no dry runs at similar obstacles for the invading soldiers.

For its part, the German army had rehearsed the defence of the region and was accurate in an assessment that the *bocage* was a bonus for the defenders. They had the luxury of camouflaged firing positions while Allied troops had to enter fields singly through small gaps, not knowing what was going to greet them the other side. This took enormous courage and there were few volunteers to step forward first. Unsurprisingly many soldiers chose to bolster their resolve with liberal quantities of calvados, the local apple brandy given out freely by a grateful local population. In places the effects of calvados were believed to be almost as damaging to the Allied thrust as enemy action.

Allied tanks were at first entirely useless against the *bocage*. As they tried to run through the lines of hedges the tank's soft underside was exposed to fire, putting its crew at huge risk. Soon engineers improvised mighty metal cutters fashioned out of beach obstacles for the front of tanks. The misery of fighting in the *bocage* did much to diminish the morale of men who felt they had done their bit for the war effort on the beaches.

One enduring shaft of sunlight for the invaders was the ability to call up air support, an option not open to the Germans suffering a chronic shortage of planes, pilots and fuel. When the Allied bombers were on target they could smash fortified gun emplacements and soften up defending towns and villages. German soldiers who were not left injured or dead were fre-

Bocage country

29 July 1944: US infantrymen advance at the double across machine-gunned ground towards enemy positions held by SS troops.

On the Alert

British troops on the hunt for snipers amidst the ruins of Le Bijudo, Caen. Although on the retreat, the German army and SS fought tenaciously for every inch of ground.

quently too numb or dazed to continue a fightback having been trapped in a firestorm of ordnance. Of course, there were occasions when the bombs fell off target and on top of fellow fighters, wreaking havoc and no small amount of fury on the ground.

As dawn broke on 7 June, or D-Day plus one, the Allies were not united at some depth over a fifty mile plus stretch of coast as planners had hoped. Troops from Gold and Juno beaches had joined forces and were close to those from Sword beach. Utah beach and pockets of territory beyond it were in Allied hands but those troops on Omaha had made small, painful progress, well short of the amount intended. All the men were exhausted from lack of sleep. That said they still enjoyed the benefits of naval gunfire. This barrage helped to keep the Germans at bay and the beaches open so that supplies of men, food, fuel, tanks and ammunition could be replenished. The resistance at Bayeux, the historic northern city, proved negligible and the place was liberated that day virtually unscathed.

Reporter Bill Downs discussed the local response:

'Everyone who has one has dug out a tricolour flag and the whole town is spotted with British flags from goodness knows where . . . But it cannot be called riotous welcome. It is more of a welcome with reservations – the reservations are only a mile and a half away. The booming of German guns and the stutter of their

machine guns are reminders to these people who have lived under the gun for some four years that liberation takes some getting used to – and it has to be made to stick. 'You can't blame them for these reservations. But our armour and our goodwill are slowly convincing them this is not a Dunkirk operation and not a Dieppe raid. 'The peculiar thing about this battle is that the French civilians are doing their best to ignore it. Not six streets from where a machine gun was operating the residents of Bayeux were having their afternoon coffee and children were playing in the streets.'

French civilians' confidence in the sticking power of the invasion was at last endorsed when the Free French leader General Charles de Gaulle arrived for a victorious walkabout within a week of liberation.

The Americans at Cherbourg

Rather than take Cherbourg from the sea Eisenhower had agreed to the American forces forging a path from the east to the west of the peninsular and sweeping upwards, placing the port under siege. It was 18 June before the finger of land was isolated by American troops even though Rommel himself conceded there was nothing that could be done to save Cherbourg and the Cotentin Peninsula, especially as the port's defenders were short of ammunition.

The Germans were stretched by the

US Advance
US artillery troops advance over ground strewn with the corpses of German soldiers and cattle in an orchard outside Cherbourg.

seeping action of Allied troops on the ground and struggled to know how to plug the advance. Aircraft pinned down German columns during daylight hours so ultimately convoys were only moving under cover of darkness. Deeper into France and Germany, aircraft bombing raids and the explosive feats of the French resistance were further disrupting the supply network. It seemed that the fall of Cherbourg and then Normandy was only a matter of time. Still Cherbourg held out. Both the Reich and Allied masterminds had identified Caen, a city split by the River Orne, as a crucial lynch pin in the battle for Normandy. Thus both sides were heavily committed to, respectively, holding or capturing the town.

Montgomery at Caen

Montgomery's forces were first split by the 21st Panzer Division when it swiftly reached the Normandy coast. The 21st Panzer Division was backed up by the 12th SS-Panzer Division Hitlerjugend, an ultra-patriotic and very able group of soldiers. British and Canadian troops were hounded by them in the first week of the campaign.

Some German tank commanders were also one step ahead in the strategy game. Montgomery's 7th Armoured Division ventured into Villers-Bocage, an important staging post en route to Caen, only to be unceremoniously ousted after a calamitous ambush by 501st SS Heavy Tank Battalion, an elite unit equipped with the fearsome Tiger tank, and commanded by

Tiger in Normandy

Soldiers of the elite SS Division Leibstandarte, *with their Panzer Mk VI Tiger E. The Tiger tank was the superior tank of the Western Front, and posed a serious threat to British and American troops.*

Doodlebug
V-1 flying bomb – an unmanned aircraft loaded with explosives – in flight. These weapons would wreak havoc on London, but would have been more damaging to the Allied war effort had they been deployed in France.

the Panzer ace *Obersturmführer* Michael Wittman on 12 June.

Rommel and Field Marshal Gerd von Rundstedt persuaded Hitler to visit France to help assess the situation. On 17 June near Soissons, on the outskirts of Paris, Rommel outlined his shrewd reading of the invaders, that they would take Caen then break out towards Paris. His proposed response was to regroup the German divisions and attack in the flanks.

One witness, General Speidel, described Hitler as 'looking worn and sleepless, playing nervously with his spectacles and an array of coloured pencils, which he held between his fingers. He was the only one who sat, hunched upon a stool, while the Field Marshals stood.'

Wonder Weapons

The Führer was barely noticing the words of the experienced Field Marshal. His thoughts were with the V1 'doodlebug' flying bombs, and the jet bombers that he believed would bring back air supremacy to Germany. Those words that did filter through to Hitler said to him 'defeatism' and he consequently refused to permit crucial troop movements requested by Rommel, sternly warning the Field Marshal about his attitude. Punished for his realism, von Rundstedt was eventually compelled to relinquish his command, to be replaced by the more compliant Field Marshal Gunther von Kluge.

The first V1 bomb – the V stood for *Vergeltungswaffe*, meaning 'reprisal weapon'– had been launched four days previously. The weapon had been developed at the secret base of Peenemunde and was designed not only to maximise casualties but also terror among the civilian population. The rocket powered Me163 Komet and the Messerschmitt Me 262, a turbojet engine plane of a newer generation than those in the Allied ranks, were at that time being primed for action and flew in sorties by Autumn 1944. Having flown the Me262 German ace Adolf Galland declared it was 'like flying on the wings of anger' and believed that one jet aircraft was equal to five conventional fighters. A new generation tank and multi barrelled gun were also in development.

Warbird

Messerschmitt Me262, the German jet-powered fighter which made its appearance in 1945.

Hitler was investing all his hopes of snatching victory from the jaws of defeat in the Peenemunde weapons programme, convinced the devastation they would wreak would force the Allies to re-assess their strategy. Word of a wonder weapon maintained many Germans' confidence in Hitler's ability to deliver a knock-out blow to his enemies at a time when others had a growing conviction in his fallibility.

The V1 bomb galvanised a British public, which had been bracing itself for some manner of retribution by Hitler. Now the fear was that he would try to win in Normandy by taking out London. To the untutored eye the V1 seemed like a small, unmanned aircraft, just 26 ft long with a wing span of 16 ft. Within its body there was 1,800 lb of explosive. Launched from ramps it achieved speeds in the order of 375 miles per hour before the engine cut out and it fell to earth. On 12 June ten V1s were launched but only four reached British soil. Just one landed in London, where it killed six people. However, the menace grew as 100 a day were soon dispatched towards Britain. Writer Evelyn Waugh described them 'as impersonal as a plague, as though the city were infested with enormous, venomous insects'. A second mass evacuation of mothers and children got underway.

The doodlebug or buzzbomb, as it was dubbed in Britain, came with a warning. When the sound of its engines ceased there were only moments to go before an explosion. Its successor, the long range V2 rocket, first launched in September was a silent killer, travelling to its target at 3,000 miles per hour bearing a one ton warhead. When the first one hit the ground in Chiswick, West London, on 9 September the tremor could be felt for miles. RAF pilots did their best to shoot the missiles out of the sky, away from built up areas.

Allied air command was at first perplexed by the rockets, or more specifically, their well protected launch sites. New 12,000lb bombs, known as Tallboys, were deployed by the RAF to smash through the reinforced concrete bunkers in which the V rockets were harboured. American fliers tried packing old planes with explosives then flying them to a fixed point and bailing out, leaving the empty, charged aircraft to be guided by remote control to the target. The experiment resulted in the loss of a number of pilots who died when the planes exploded prematurely, among them Joseph Kennedy Jr, older brother of future American president John F Kennedy.

About 8,000 V1s rained down on England until Allied troops overran the launch sites some three months after D-Day. The effect of the bombs might have been much worse if the Germans had not been hampered in their production by perpetual air raids. Likewise production of the V2 was sporadic. The value of the weapons in the end proved greater to America than to Hitler, as bomb maker in chief Wernher von Braun was whisked off to the States after the war to help develop its rocket and space programmes.

At the time of the Soissons summit Hitler's faith in the V1 must have been badly shaken by its apparent lack of impact that week, although Josef Goebbels, the Third Reich's propaganda master, told Germany the missiles had set the capital ablaze and sent its residents fleeing.

It was Hitler himself who dealt a blow to the effectiveness of the Me262 by demanding it had bomber as well as fighter capability. That personal order delayed its mass production until the war was all but lost. Had it appeared in combat against Allied bombers and fighters early in 1944 it might have overwhelmed the opposition and regained the initiative for the Luftwaffe.

On the stocks also was the V3, a multi-barrelled gun capable of firing 300lb shells across the Channel at a rate of one every six seconds. Stuttering though the Allied advance was, it proved sufficiently swift to knock out launch sites for the rockets and destabilise the weapons programme. In a different time frame, though, the weapons would have significantly protracted the war, especially if the new planes deprived the Allies of air superiority. Had he thoroughly understood the trump card of nuclear warheads Hitler might have propelled his scientists in a different direction, with devastating results. As it was, Germany was stuck in something of a weapons rut following D-Day and was still reliant in the region on horse-drawn artillery.

At sea the German navy seemed largely impotent in the week following D-Day when the Channel was throbbing with invasion traffic. U-boats and torpedo boats had some limited success with small boats but lost two of their number to British anti-submarine forces.

Napoleon once asked for the army to yield generals that were lucky. German commanders might well have bemoaned their joint misfortunes as the D-Day cam-

Open Fire

British patrol defends a roadblock with a grenade launcher, July 1944. The enemy is just 200 yards forward of their position.

paign unfolded. Yet the Allied troops were none too lucky either and continued to experience problems that were not of their own making.

On 19 June the weather threw up the worst storms in 40 years and gales wrecked the Mulberry harbours that had been in situ for just three days, severely disrupting the landing of supplies. Until that point the Mulberry serving the American beach had alone permitted the movement of daily cargo amounting to about 14,500 tons. It wasn't until 29 June that the Mulberry harbour at Arromanches was back in commission while the one at Omaha beach, where 600 vehicles had also been destroyed, was deemed beyond repair. The problems of landing supplies were compounded by what occurred at Cherbourg.

Despite the fact that his men were cut off without hope of relief before the end of June, Hitler had exhorted that the port should be defended to the last man and 'leave to the enemy not a harbour but a field of ruins'. However, with American troops on land and Allied ships providing a barrage from the sea, there was little point in mounting a sacrifice-all defence. Cherbourg's commander General Karl-Wilhelm von Schlieben tried to acquiesce to the demands of both Hitler and the Americans by giving himself up while refusing to surrender the port. But as German soldiers saw their leader jump from a sinking ship they followed suit and surrendered. The port, such as it was, fell into Allied hands. When the Americans finally entered Cherbourg they found all the port facilities comprehensively wrecked and it would be some time before the Allies could run in and out of the captured harbour at will. At least the fuel pipe PLUTO came on line by the end of June, pumping 8,000 tons of petrol per day from Britain.

The Americans now looked south to the communications crossroads of St Lo. Hopes that it would be an easy target were false, though, as the soldiers were faced with mile after mile of tedious *bocage.*

Operation *Epsom*

To the east, Montgomery was experiencing a start-stop campaign that was also prey to the poor weather. Operation *Epsom* began on 26 June following a three day delay caused by the weather. Montgomery's intention was to push south and then east in a semi-circle in mostly open country to take the high ground around Caen. He opened with an artillery barrage and limited air support. Some of the bitterest fighting yet seen occurred. However, the 11th Armoured Division installed tanks on Hill 112, trying to control the high ground that might eventually lead to control of the bridges on the River Orne. Scottish soldiers were also prominent in the action. Later, all were forced to withdraw although there was little contest at that time from the enemy. Veteran Albert Figg reveals the unexpected retreat was called for by Montgomery after German codes were secretly read at Bletchley Park, revealing that three Panzer divisions were advancing with orders to attack Hill 112. Stiff resistance and the expectation of more ultimately brought the operation to an end although German armour had been tied up for its duration.

On 4 July the Canadian 3rd Division weighed in with Operation *Windsor,* its objective being to capture the village of Carpiquet and its strategically important airfield. Support came from the guns of HMS *Rodney*, anchored off the coast, and rocket-firing Typhoon fighter aircraft. Had it succeeded, the western approaches to Caen would have been cleared. As it was, the Canadians were only partially successful and bore heavy losses as the tenacious 12th SS Panzer Division held fast during a two day onslaught.

On 7 July the Allied strategic bombers came at the request of forces who were in a rut as they tried to take Caen. Some 2,300 tons of bombs were dropped on the northern sector of the city by 457 RAF planes, reducing the area to ruins. The action enabled the infantry to advance, but the bomb craters it caused stopped tanks and armoured vehicles in their tracks. Soldiers were then deprived of protection as they picked their way through the smoking rubble and were vulnerable to enemy snipers during house-to-house fighting. The wrecked city was finally taken with an alarming number of Allied casualties but Germans withdrew to strong defensive positions across the river nearby, still able to harass Allied columns if they tried to push on.

Three days later Operation *Jupiter* was launched with the intention of reclaiming Hill 112, given up in June with few casualties. The human cost of winning it back would be great. During the intervening days the Germans had fortified their newly assumed positions, appreciating the importance of a hill that gave clear views up to the coast and across to Caen. In a desperate struggle the 43rd Wessex Division held the hill for 48 hours before being beaten back by two Panzer divisions. The casualties among the Wessex division alone in that time amounted to 2,000 – and the battle for the hill was unresolved. Nominal control changed hands several times before the fighting came to an end, with the wooded summit becoming a 'no man's land'.

Albert Figg is categoric about its importance. 'It is the battle that started the end of the war. If we had lost that hill we would have been pushed back into the sea. At the time supplies were held up due to the bad weather. Things could have gone either way.' Rommel also once said that he who holds Hill 112 controls Normandy.

Figg had joined the Territorial Army in 1939 at the age of 19, was called up into the Wessex Regiment later that year and recalls being posted to Kent following D-Day to guard against German invasion when supplies were so short that there was one rifle between a dozen men.

Mine Clearance

Tilly-sur-Seulles, 19 June: British engineers clear minefields after they captured the town. A Bren carrier destroyed by mines lies in the foreground.

He went to Normandy on 24 June, landing at Gold Beach and experiencing the terrors of descending a rope ladder from a ship to a landing craft in heaving seas. After de-waterproofing his 25lb gun the artillery man went into action in the vicinity of Bayeux station.

'Hill 112 is a piece of raised ground between the Odon and the Orne rivers. During Operation Epsom I was firing from about three miles away when all of a sudden a message came through to reduce our range considerably. Immediately I knew we had been firing at our own troops.'

Part of a six man team operating the gun, Figg was then called into seemingly incessant action again during *Jupiter* when the bloodshed was worse.

'As a gunner you don't see your target. We were called the five mile snipers. This time I was at Carpiquet, about three and a half miles away from Hill 112. During the 12 day battle my regiment (112 Field Regiment) fired some 65,000 shells from 24 guns. With the rest of the fire power trained on it there must have been close on 1,000 tons of high explosive falling every day on Hill 112.

'My division was the main attack force gathered at the start line. We had at our disposal the support of heavy armour from the tank regiments assigned to us. The tanks, British-built Churchills and American Shermans, gave us great comfort as we prepared for battle.

'To our horror we were to find out that our supporting tanks were no match for the mighty German Tiger 1. Out gunned and out armoured, our tanks were turned into infernos. The Germans nicknamed the Sherman 'Ronson' because it would go up in flames if hit, just like a Ronson lighter.

'In one day alone fifty Churchills were 'brewed up', with many of the crews being killed. The expression 'brewed up' was the way a soldier could sanitise and so cope with the horrendous way many tankmen died. Many were trapped inside the hull of the tank to be consumed by fire, screaming for help in the full knowledge that no one in the heat of battle could hear them, let alone do anything to help them.'

To honour the courage of the tank crews and the 7,000 casualties of Hill 112, Figg and fellow members of the 43rd Wessex Association campaigned to place a Churchill tank atop the summit. It was unveiled 55 years after the battle. He also remembers small-scale tragedies, like the death of a British soldier the day before he was due to go on leave after his wife had given birth to twins. He was killed when a fellow Tommy dropped his Sten gun, letting loose a spray of bullets.

This section of the Normandy campaign was a test of endurance both for Allied and German soldiers. For the Allies also it was a great strain on the supply chain, as massive quantities of ammunition and tanks were needed to replace those being destroyed.

Then came Operation *Goodwood*, conceived in part by Lieutenant-General Sir Miles Dempsey, a close associate of Montgomery and commander of the Second Army. Preceded by air attacks, it began on 18 July with the aim of reaching into Falaise, flatter countryside more suited to armoured vehicles that promised rapid progress for the invaders. The massive aerial onslaught helped to secure a fast start for troops and tanks. The offensive did end with Caen being cleared of German soldiers – 36 days after D-Day when it was earmarked to fall – and an advance of some three miles (five km) towards Falaise. But there it came to a halt with a mighty counter attack led by German anti-tank guns poised on the Bourguebus Ridge. The operation was finally called off when a fierce summer storm on 20 July further compromised British troops. Gains were slight while losses amounted to some 4,000 men and 500 tanks, more than a third of the total possessed by the British in Normandy at the time.

Montgomery claimed the intention was to occupy the attentions of the key Panzer units so the US advance could continue unhindered by them. His detractors were not so sure, believing one of the operations at least was an attempt to break out that had badly failed.

Montgomery's command became the subject of scrutiny as several efforts to make the British presence in the region come to nothing. Afterwards Major Chester Hansen, who worked with both Eisenhower and Montgomery, revealed: 'He was a good commander in set metal situations. In a mobile situation we thought he was rather slow to move and tidy up the battlefield. Perhaps if we had been in the war as long as the British and taken the casualties they had we would have been a lot more cautious too.'

On the positive side, if gains were slight there was no sign of the Allies being dislodged. More men and supplies were feeding into the battle from the beaches. The First Canadian Army led by General Henry Crerar came into Montgomery's operational sphere on 23 July while General George S Patton brought his Third US Army into action on 1 August. As Rommel feared, once the British, American and Canadian armies gained a solid foothold on the Continent it would be doubly difficult to evict them.

One unscheduled spin-off to Montgomery's operation was the elimination from the field of his old North African adversary Rommel. After visiting a Panzer unit in Caen Rommel was the passenger in a car driven from the road by strafing from Allied planes on 17 July. He suffered a fractured skull and was unable to continue in his capacity as commander.

The 20 July Bomb Plot

For the Germans this was a blow, but paled into insignificance against the sensational news that emerged from Germany three days later. An audacious attempt to assassinate Hitler had taken place as the Führer met with his military chiefs at his East Prussian headquarters. It was not the first plan to eliminate Hitler but probably came the closest to succeeding. A leading player in the plot, Claus von Stauffenberg, carried a bomb into the meeting primed to explode after he himself had slipped out. Von Stauffenberg was a veteran of German fronts in Poland, France, Russia and Africa. It was while he was in Tunisia that he was injured, losing his left eye, right hand and two fingers from his left hand. As the conflict continued, he became convinced Hitler would bring Germany to disaster. Nevertheless he still cut an aristocratic and authoritative figure in the German hierarchy and retained the trust of the Führer.

When he slipped into the high level meeting von Stauffenberg placed the briefcase with its fuse already started beneath a large oak table spread with

The Aftermath

A shaken Hitler shows the visiting Mussolini his devastated bunker in the Wolf's Lair headquarters at Rastenburg in Prussia.

maps and documents. On the pretext of making a telephone call to Berlin he left – and moments later was rewarded by the sounds of a hefty explosion.

Yet beyond all expectation, Hitler came staggering out of the smoking debris with comparatively minor injuries. He soon turned the incident into a propaganda coup, claiming his survival was a sign that destiny intended him to rule the western world. His first visitor was Benito Mussolini on a scheduled trip, having been kicked out of Italy as Allied troops consolidated their gains there. Both men agreed that fate must have taken a hand. In a radio broadcast later that evening Hitler affirmed: 'I regard this as a fresh confirmation of the mission given me by Providence to continue toward my goal.'

Von Stauffenberg, meanwhile, had taken a plane to Berlin where he and other conspirators began to take control of the government of Germany. Convinced their target must have been obliterated, they took the first tentative steps towards overturning Nazism. But a hesitancy born from years of unquestioning loyalty to the dictator cost them dearly. Hitler was soon on the telephone to countermand the orders issued by the high-ranking plotters. The game was up almost before it began.

The high profile officers involved, including von Stauffenberg, were executed immediately on the orders of General Fromm in Berlin, who realised his own head might be on the line if his compliance with the men was revealed. They were the lucky ones. A vicious manhunt began which resulted in others involved being hanged with piano wire upon meat hooks, a gruesome sight allegedly filmed for Hitler's consumption.

It sparked an atmosphere of unprecedented paranoia in the Reich that did little to help its cause in the field. Hitler became more than ever convinced that the army generals were not to be trusted and that his judgement alone should be brought to bear. As for Rommel, it is likely he would have joined the conspirators had they been successful and had he been well, and perhaps ended the battle for Normandy that very day. As it was, his distant association with von Stauffenberg was sufficient to sign his death warrant. He chose to commit suicide to spare his family public humiliation. When his death ultimately occurred on 14 October it was reported that he died in a car crash. The 53-year old Rommel had been the Third Reich's most successful general: his troops in Normandy would feel his absence in the months ahead.

Operation *Cobra*

Anxious to prevent the arrival of Panzer units in his theatre of operations, General Bradley devised Operation *Cobra* to spring American troops out of St Lo. As the American forces headed south west they would drive the German forces to the Atlantic coast. Bad weather on 20 July grounded the bombers that he needed for the obliteration of earmarked targets. There was a four-day delay before it could unfold, offering the Germans the valuable gift of time. Then, like the British operations, it ran into costly blips and hitches but was more clearly defined and largely successful.

The folly of carpet bombing in the vicinity of home troops was underlined forcefully during Operation *Cobra* when two friendly fire incidents in as many days claimed the lives of 136 American servicemen, among them Lieutenant-General Lesley McNair, the highest ranking Allied officer to be killed in the Normandy campaign. More than 620 were wounded.

The first attack, involving 1,900 bombers carrying 3,950 tons of bombs, was described by Major General Fritz Bayerlein, whose men were the intended targets.

'The planes kept coming over as if on a conveyor belt and the bomb carpets unrolled in great rectangles.

'My flak had hardly opened its mouth when the batteries received direct hits which knocked out half the guns and silenced the rest. After an hour I had no communication with anybody, even by radio. By noon nothing was visible but dust and smoke.'

Afterwards Eisenhower ruled that carpet bombing was to be used against German installations rather than for close ground support.

Meanwhile, German soldiers fighting in Normandy made a grim joke of the lack of air support available to them. They claimed that a silver aircraft overhead belonged to the Americans; a dark

Safe Return

Bomber crews of the US Ninth Airforce leave their B26 Marauder aircraft after returning from a mission to support the D-Day landings in Normandy by disrupting German lines of communication and supply.

coloured aircraft was British. If it couldn't be seen at all, it was German.

Close-quarter combat continued and sniper fire remained a potent threat to Allied troops. However on 31 July the US broke through at Avranches, in a successful conclusion to Bradley's Operation *Cobra*. For the British and Canadians progress remained slight.

There was also utter confusion on the ground as the front line separating Allied and German troops fluctuated by the hour. Peter Strachan, from the 147th Brigade of the Royal Army Signal Corps, explained how he spent a night sleeping with the enemy.

'Unknown to me, the Germans had pushed us back. I was driving along according to a map reference I had been given. It was pitch dark amongst some trees. I saw some trenches about 50 yards long. They looked nice and safe so I stopped the truck and hopped in one to get some kip. I saw shadows further up, about 30 yards away. They didn't talk and I didn't talk. I dozed off. As day broke these shadows moved off. Some men in the British infantry later came up

and asked what I was doing. "You shouldn't be here," they told me, explaining that the area – and the trench itself – had been in the hands of the Germans overnight.'

If the faltering progress of the Allies surprised the public it came as no shock to Roosevelt who, on 6 June, had predicted for the troops a long and hard road in the face of a strong enemy. 'He may hurl back our forces. Success may not come with rushing speed. But we shall return again and again.'

Savagery of the SS

As the Battle for Normandy unfolded it was to be the backdrop for some cold-blooded murders. On 8 June as Canadian forces began one of numerous attempts to take Caen, about 40 men were taken prisoner by soldiers of the 2nd Battalion of the 26th SS-Panzer Grenadier Regiment commanded by Wilhelm Mohnke, a man who already had form for his part in the slaughter of British prisoners of war trying to reach Dunkirk in 1940. The unlucky Canadians were marched into a field and shot by guards using machine guns. Five men escaped to tell the tale. It is believed the same SS group killed six Canadians at a first aid post in the vicinity.

A further three Canadian prisoners were executed at Forme du Bosq, Mohnke's headquarters, as the callous commander stood and watched.

The action taken by Germans against the residents of the small French village of Oradour-sur-Glane near Limoges is a measure of the panic that was running through at least a few of the Nazi commanders. On 10 June 1944, many miles south of the Normandy battle zone, the village's men were locked into a barn and slaughtered in a hail of bullets by troops from the elite SS *Das Reich* division. For women and children the destination was the church. When the doors were locked with the innocents on the inside SS troops fired explosives into the building and pumped bullets through doors and windows. Heat from the inferno was so intense that the church bells melted and the 450 inside didn't stand a chance. Just seven villagers survived.

At first it seemed the atrocity was committed as a reprisal for resistance activity in the area. There was a theory that German crack troops were so frustrated with delays and incompetence in their own ranks that they vented their anger on the village. Later another explanation emerged, that a convoy of Nazi loot had been attacked and stolen and senior officers in the SS were anxious for its return. They presumed the residents of Oradour were involved but, when no information about the theft was forthcoming, they wanted no potential witnesses left alive. Oradour has been preserved as it was left by the SS as a memorial for those who died and a reminder of the brutality that scarred parts of Europe during the era.

Losses were high and while much had been achieved, there was still plenty to do. The road that began at the Normandy beaches ended in Berlin. The enduring task weighed with soldiers whose mood fluctuated from triumphant and proud to mutinous. One BBC report used the words of an RAF Wing Commander, L Nickolls, to describe the lot of the British Tommy in Normandy.

'I think one of the things I shall never forget is the sight of the British infantry, plodding steadily up those dusty French

The Town that Died
The French town of Oradour. Destroyed by Waffen-SS troops of the Das Reich *division, the town has been left as a memorial to its unfortunate inhabitants.*

roads towards the front, single-file, heads bent down against the heavy weight of the kit piled on their backs, armed to the teeth, they were plodding on, slowly and doggedly to the front with the sweat running down their faces and enamel drinking mugs dangling at their hips, never looking back and hardly ever looking to the side – just straight ahead and down a little at the roughness of the road, while the jeeps and the lorries and the tanks and all the other traffic went crowding by, smothering them in great billows and clouds of dust which they never even deigned to notice. That was a sight that somehow caught at your heart . . .'

As a constant reminder of the scale of sacrifice in Northern France there are the war cemeteries spread through the region. In each Allied cemetery there are rows upon rows upon rows of white crosses (American) or white headstones (British and Commonwealth), each bearing a name, a rank and outfit and a date, underlining the fact that the killing continued from 6 June throughout the summer months as Allied troops struggled to bring Normandy back into the free world. Interred are the bodies of men from Manchester, Montreal and Mississippi who were linked by one heroic but personally disastrous attack to change the course of history. The cemeteries are kept fresh and neatly manicured as a tribute to those who gave their lives. Equally poignant are the German cemeteries containing the bodies of those who died defending the Reich, minnows caught up in a mighty tide.

CHAPTER FOUR

The Destruction of Warsaw

'I would like to make an appeal to the British nation. It is short: HELP FOR WARSAW.'

Flight Lieutenant John Ward at the Warsaw Uprising

On 1 August 1944, the patriotic Polish Home Army began an uprising against Nazi rule in Warsaw with sufficient ammunition to last for 12 days. Its supporters did so knowing that Red Army soldiers were within sight of the city, squatting across the River Vistula. Regular bursts of gunfire reassured them that the Russian spring offensive had powered down towards the Polish capital and was pressing German forces into an ignominious retreat.

England and France had gone to war in 1939 when Poland was invaded by Germany. The stricken country was immediately divided between Germany and Stalin's Russia as a result of a secret pact between the two leaders that initially kept the Soviets out of the war. It was a miserable episode in Poland's chequered history. The people had endured five years of occupation by one invader or another but now the Polish dream of a nationhood was once again resurgent.

However, Stalin had no desire for democracy in Poland. Aware of anti-Soviet feeling in the country, he was opposed outright to having a strong, independent Poland on his country's border. Rather, his vision for post war Europe featured a satellite state that was itself dependent on the largesse of Mother Russia for survival. This would be a part of a barrier to defend Soviet Russia against future attacks from the west.

Consequently, when the uprising began with 150,000 men and women taking to the streets of Warsaw the Red Army stood by and did nothing. When German troops refused to withdraw and indeed fought viciously to suppress the insurgency Russian soldiers did not intervene – even though the Poles were ostensibly allies.

Stalin's Reaction

With a little forethought it would not have been hard to gauge Stalin's response. He had previously refused to recognise the Polish Home Army (also known as the Armija Krajowa or AK), and had already broken off relations with the Polish government in exile. (His slaughter of 4,400 Polish officers at Katyn Wood was at the time believed to be the work of the Germans.) He believed he had won backing from other Allied leaders at the Tehran conference in 1943 for Russia to take a portion of Poland after hostilities equivalent to that awarded under the 1939 agreement with Hitler. Had the Home Army hesitated for a moment they might

have realised their cause would not win Soviet backing. However, their nationalist fervour proved too powerful to contain.

Churchill and Roosevelt were caught in an awkward position. Both were keen to assist the freedom fighters in Poland but they did not wish to upset their Russian ally and so risk the overall game plan, which was the total defeat of Germany by a united Allied force. It was difficult to disprove outright Stalin's word on the Warsaw issue, that his army was facing unexpectedly tough German opposition in the region, and there was a mighty reluctance to become involved in what was essentially a neighbourhood dispute. Churchill did in fact make some diplomatic efforts on Poland's behalf.

But in the face of appeals from Churchill and the Polish prime minister in exile Mikolajczyk, Stalin dismissed the situation in Warsaw as 'exaggerated and

March of Death

Captured Jewish civilians who participated in Jewish ghetto uprisings are marched out of the city by Nazi troops, Warsaw, Poland, 19 April, 1943. The Poles would rise again in 1944, only to be crushed once more.

misleading'. Later, when the British and American governments asked for permission to use Soviet airfields to drop much-needed supplies to the Polish fighters Stalin branded the uprising as 'a reckless adventure'. The necessary permission was not forthcoming. Although Polish patriots fought from street to house and sewer with suicidal gallantry, German troops, often commanded by unsavoury characters such as SS-*Brigadeführer* Oskar Dirlewanger, a convicted sex criminal, proceeded to put down the uprising with appalling barbarity. Residents, dazed by the perpetual sound of gunfire, were reduced to eating horse and dog meat.

Eyewitness Testimony

London was made aware of the atrocities taking place in Warsaw after the uprising by Flight Lieutenant John Ward, an RAF wireless operator and an escapee from a German prisoner of war camp, who pitched up in Warsaw to fight with the Home Army.

In August 1944 he filed a report from Warsaw revealing: 'About 40 per cent of the city centre is already completely destroyed. The German forces make no difference between civilians and troops of the Home Army.' Later he told how a German panzer column used 500 Polish women and children as human shields.

As the situation deteriorated for the Home Army he wrote: 'Sir, the main things needed are grenades, anti-tank weapons, heavy machine guns, rifles, ammunition of all types.

A week later: 'Poland is a country which I, as an Englishman, am proud to call an ally. She produced no government to co-operate with the Germans . . . To this end I would like to make an appeal to the British nation. It is short: HELP FOR WARSAW.'

The Poles had a fundamental faith in the British government, which indeed continued attempts to assist in a small way. However, when relief flights from Brindisi in Italy flew to Warsaw they were shot at by Soviet forces. As a result the Allies kept their distance while the Polish cause became ever more hopeless.

On 2 October, two months after the revolt kicked off, the German army claimed victory in its comprehensive repression of Warsaw as the artillery-weary Polish inhabitants surrendered. The death toll was huge. About 500,000 residents were deported and immediately afterwards an estimated 85 per cent of the city was razed. To their credit the Germans treated the Poles as combatants – meaning they were destined for prisoner of war camps – rather than partisans, which would have meant instant death.

A Nation Abandoned?

When Russians finally liberated the city in January 1945 they discovered just 162,000 people had returned alive out of a pre-war population of 1,310,000, all emaciated with hunger and sheltering in the ruins of what was once an architecturally fine place. Poland – losing one fifth of its population during World War Two – had contributed greatly to the Allied cause by providing valuable information both about the German encoding machine and the V1 bombs. Its people showed relentless kindness to prisoners of war held in Polish territory, often sharing meagre rations when they themselves were starving. Only a few Polish people were guilty of collaborating with the occupying Germans. The belief that Poland was let

down by its allies in the Second World War is still an enduring one, even today. Curiously, in 2004 it was German Chancellor Gerhard Schröder who issued a public apology to the Poles. At 5pm on 1 August 2004 – exactly 60 years to the hour after the uprising began – Mr Schröder laid a wreath in memory of the 250,000 Poles who died in the 63-day long battle. (Chancellor Schröder's own father, Lance Corporal Fritz Schröder, died in October 1944 fighting against the Red Army in Rumania when the Chancellor was six months old.)

Ghetto Resistance

Members of the Polish Home Army begin to fight back against the German occupiers. Their brave uprising would end in tragedy, however.

CHAPTER FIVE

The Falaise Pocket

Allied aircraft formed queues to fire at 'sitting duck' columns, destroying thousands of vehicles a day

The Allied inaction was all the more bitter given that a sizeable number of Poles were fighting against Germany in the on-going Normandy campaign. In addition to Polish, British, Canadian and American troops there were also Australians, New Zealanders, Czechoslovakians, the Free Dutch, Greeks, Norwegians, some Irish, the Free French and German anti-fascists.

In the German ranks there were Rumanians, Russians, Hungarians, Ukrainians, Latvians, Lithuanians, French pro-Fascists and collaborators who fought in the Charlemagne division during the defence of Berlin. The Free India Legion, nationalists seeking to oust Britain from the sub-continent, also fought for the Germans. (Some of the above were recruited from the ranks of prisoners of war or slave labourers and believed combat was the lesser of two evils.)

Operation *Cobra* had been temporarily halted by a German counteroffensive, known as Operation *Luttich*, on 7 August at Mortain. But it quickly recovered its momentum, bringing troops south and west out of Avranches. A French division under General Philippe Leclerc (a pseudonym used to protect his family living in Occupied France) was making rapid progress from the south. Meanwhile, Canadians, Poles and British fighters were pouring down from the north in Operation *Totalize* begun on 8 August.

The Allies formulated Operation *Tractable* with the aim of encircling the German Seventh Army, which had hitherto been compelled to stay in its hopeless position by Hitler's refusal to permit withdrawal. Indeed Hitler was keen for his generals to mount a further counteroffensive against the Americans regardless of the human cost. Convinced the unfolding rout in Normandy was the fault of spinelessness or even subordination among senior officers, Hitler replaced Field Marshal von Kluge, commander in chief of operations in the west, with Field Marshal Walther Model.

The key elements of *Tractable* were known to the Germans after a Canadian officer carrying a blueprint of it was captured after being parted from his unit.

Thus the Germans identified a corridor through which to escape to the east and knew where best to mount their defences against the Allied charge. It was at a point south east of Falaise, specifically the town of Chambois, and meant crossing the River Dives. To assist, the II SS Panzer Corps – which had already

slipped out of Normandy – returned to hold open the gap, allowing as many German officers and men to flee through as possible. On 16 August the gap was 18 kilometres wide. Two days later the neck measured just eight kilometres and was still shrinking. Sensing their imminent destruction, German units forged ahead frequently overrunning or outrunning Allied patrols in their path.

The roadways and fields were the scene of a disorderly withdrawal, albeit in full view of the advancing Canadian and Polish troops perched on surrounding hills. German progress was perpetually impeded by strafing from Allied aircraft that sometimes had to form queues to take turns at firing on 'sitting duck' columns, destroying literally thousands of vehicles each day. Casualties including horses and wreckage soon gummed up the roads, slowing them still further. Wounded men were often abandoned in roadside ditches. On 19 August, the day Field Marshal Von Kluge committed suicide by taking cyanide, German troops

Into the Falaise Pocket

Canadian and British troops advance towards Falaise, on the road from Caen, 11 August 1944. The fires have been caused by heavy Allied bombing.

War Souvenir

After mopping up the last German resistance in the Falaise Gap area, US infantrymen display captured swastika flag in front of wrecked German tank.

were given the order: 'Every man for themselves.'

The Breakout

Major General Kurt Meyer was among those fleeing to the east. 'The enemy stands on the hilltops firing relentlessly into the pocket. Most of the victims belong to the infantry support units who remain in the pocket with their horse-drawn transport. Leaderless, they run for their lives.'

The action at Falaise decimated his division that had been 20,000 strong in early June with some 150 tanks at its disposal. By 25 August it had less than 300 men in its ranks and had lost all its tanks and artillery.

(Meyer was later captured and tried for the murder of Canadian prisoners in Normandy. A death sentence was commuted to life imprisonment then 14 years. He was released in 1954 and died in 1961.)

Fighting around the Falaise Gap proved to be among the most fierce and costly of the Normandy campaign. Among the Germans the corridor was known as the death road as about 10,000 of their number were killed. At least one attempt to close the pocket failed following a desperate forward thrust by the Germans. The most tenacious fighters for Reich were those from the Hitler Youth, the 12th SS-Panzer Division *Hitlerjugend.* While it wasn't pretty, the German withdrawal through the Falaise Gap was something of a military masterstroke, equivalent in terms to the British escape at Dunkirk.

In the afternoon of 21 August the pocket was finally sealed when different columns of Allied troops linked up. No more German soldiers could slip through to fight another day. Following an appeal by a French priest, a trapped German commander allowed the 150,000 men still within the confines of the pocket to surrender rather than fight to the death.

The human and material wreckage still littered the valley, though, and the stench of burning flesh filled the atmosphere. It was a sight that struck home with Allied soldiers, as the sum total of their action.

John Warner, a forward observer with 344th Field Artillery Battalion of the 90th Infantry Division witnessed what occurred and later gave his verdict on the battle for Falaise. 'What I saw in the Falaise Gap was disgusting. Revolting. I'll tell you, and I'm not ashamed to be a part of it because it was a necessity...it was a job I had to do. But I don't care who you are or what type of people you are, it's hard.'

To Allied troops now fell the tasks of sweeping for mines, burying the dead and bulldozing the twisted wreckage of equipment off the road.

There were spats between Allied commanders over why so many Germans escaped. Some of the American higher command blamed the British, believing Montgomery should have closed the Falaise gap much earlier rather than simply pressing German units from the flank to herd them into the pocket. The Allied commanders as a whole, however, were keen to cut casualties among their own men and acted accordingly. US general Omar Bradley pegged back the Americans at Argentan to prevent friendly fire incidents between themselves and the Canadians. He observed: 'I much preferred a solid shoulder at Argentan to the possibility of a broken neck at Falaise.' Was it a victory or a defeat that helped to prolong the conflict? Whatever the view, the battle for Normandy was about over. Allied troops continued to harry the retreating Germans who headed for the Seine and then for the Low Countries or Germany itself. The chase was tempered by a shortage of fuel.

There were also pockets of German resistance in the Channel ports that took time to wipe out, but these would never have seriously threatened the position of the Allies in Normandy.

CHAPTER SIX

The Liberation of Paris

The German commander of Paris, General von Choltitz, courageously ignored Hitler's orders to make of Paris 'a Stalingrad of the West', and began talks with the Resistance.

German troubles were far from finished however with an additional invasion force landing on the French Riviera on 15 August. This had originally been known as Operation *Anvil* and was scheduled to take place alongside the Normandy landings. British commanders were unenthusiastic about staging it but the Americans believed it essential. A shortage of amphibious craft meant its postponement until mid August when, re-named Operation *Dragoon*, it went ahead manned by American and Free French army divisions with the aim of opening Marseilles as a supply port. Although it was by nature a subsidiary operation, it nevertheless consisted of 880 ships and 1,370 landing craft. Some 5,000 men were parachuted behind enemy lines from the gaping jaws of 396 transport planes. The first village to be liberated in southern France was La Motte when it was taken by B company 6th Parachute Battalion.

Germans were perplexed to hear about an influx of Allied invaders at Toulon and devoted plenty of time and energy to formulating a response. In fact the 'invaders' were 600 dummy parachutists fitted with devices to mimic small arms fire.

Casualties throughout *Dragoon* were comparatively light and the invaders made gratifyingly swift progress, securing their target within eight days. It was remembered by one war correspondent, Wynford Vaughan Thomas, as the champagne campaign after he and other invaders were greeted on the beach by a Frenchman bearing a tray with a bottle of bubbly and glasses. 'Welcome, you are somewhat late,' the champagne bearer gently chided. Thereafter Allied troops began mopping up in Vichy France. It would only be a matter of time before the Allies turned their attentions to the French capital.

The Popular Uprising

In Paris the emotions that bubbled under the surface of all France were thrown into one seething cauldron. Proud and patriotic French people who had lived under the German jackboot for four years were at the end of their tether. For them the occupation was nothing short of shameful. Then there were others who shared the Nazi's anti-Semitic sentiments and co-operated with them. Those who were once grateful of a leg-up in the administrative structure imposed by the occupying Germans grew more fearful as the potency of Hitler's regime ebbed away. Awaiting them was the venom of the

On the Barricades

Encouraged by the sound of Allied artillery around the city, the citizens of Paris take up arms against the German army of occupation.

Resistance, the small but vociferous urban and rural terrorists who conducted secret operations against German troops under threat of terrible consequences. No one knows precisely the numbers that acted in the French Resistance, but one broadly accepted estimate deems that in 1943 some 100,000 people were under the umbrella of the organisation. Once unleashed no one was sure who would reel the resistance in again. Communists wearing hammer and sickle armbands also sought revenge. Caught up in the onslaught of anti-German feelings were ordinary people who had done business with Germans because it was the only business to be had. There were women who dated Germans because there was no one else who was eligible and women who saw to the sexual needs of German soldiers

as a way to feed their children. Some even fell in love. A whole raft of the population collaborated to maintain a comfortable lifestyle. But by August 1944 one feeling among the French went over and above that of fear, frustration or lust for revenge. It was hunger.

Life under German occupation might have trimmed the personal freedom of the French population, and wounded their pride, but it had not unduly affected the contents of their larders. Following the D-Day invasion the supply of provisions from rural Normandy into the city had been abruptly halted. Likewise, supplies of produce from Vichy France had also dried up. The arrival of liberating troops meant an end to deprivation and this alone would ensure a warm welcome for Allied soldiers. By the middle of August,

Paris Liberated

American infantry troops march in triumph down the Champs Elysee after liberating Paris, August 1944.

the Allies were so close to Paris that liberation would surely come in a matter of weeks. In fact the Parisiennes decided they could not wait that long.

On hearing the reassuring boom of Allied gunfire on the city limits, the Resistance began an uprising in Paris on 19 August in which the desperate, dedicated French threw themselves, ill-armed and untrained, against the occupying German forces. The result was only going one way, given the proximity of the Free French army, closely followed by the Americans.

Yet many patriots died in the street fights, and no one could take away from the Resistance a tremendous victory that helped to expunge four years of humiliation. An Allied decision to delay the liberation of Paris so as to avoid inflicting civilians casualties was reversed and General Leclerc sent forward an armoured division which arrived on the outskirts on 24 August. That same evening Charles de Gaulle took a triumphant walk along the Champs Elysees regardless of the remaining threat of German sniper fire.

On 25 August 1944 Parisian church bells tolled to signify the end of German occupation. For the most part the population was euphoric, prompting Simone de Beauvoir to call the response 'an orgy of fraternity'. Collaborators, however, were fearful of the inevitable reprisals. For women guilty of '*collaboration horizontale*' this meant being stripped and having their heads shaved on the street. They were daubed with their own blood and swastikas and paraded before contemptuous neighbours. The women were then ostracised while their illegitimate children were publicly taunted for years afterwards.

Mob justice was especially severe for those whose denouncement of a friend or neighbour to the German authorities had ended in tragedy. The worst was reserved for members of the militia armed by the Germans who carried out operations during the occupation against the resistance.

Across France the stories of revenge taken against collaborators occasionally filtered into the local press. Impossible now to verify, there were tales of one pensioner priest having his nails and hair torn out and his ribs shattered. Another priest was forced to dig his own grave and was then buried alive after being shot in the genitals. Alarmed by the prospect of civil conflict on his watch, Charles de Gaulle ordered an investigation after the war that found 4,167 summary executions of Frenchmen by Frenchmen took place after D-Day. In January 1945 French police dealt with 42 executions, 122 armed attacks and 151 bombings that occurred as a result of D-Day and the ensuing liberation. The issue of collaboration – who did it and how they were punished – was swept under the carpet for generations.

By way of a footnote, Paris owes a debt of gratitude to its erstwhile German commander General Dietrich von Choltitz. He was the unlikely and unsung hero of the hour, albeit one who was taken in an open top car with his head bowed, a broken man, to sign the surrender.

Four days prior to this public humbling, Choltitz had been expressly ordered by Hitler to burn Paris. Hitler called for the city to be reduced to 'a pile of rubble', the fate of Warsaw before the Germans withdrew. As always there was the hidden agenda, that substantial rafts of the population should die.

As he gazed around at the elegant

architecture, the broad boulevards and splendid bridges Choltitz must have been in turmoil. Should he obey without question the Führer he had been conditioned for a dozen years to love and honour? Or was the beauty of the city a matter quite apart from modern politics and warfare? Choltitz listened to that small inner voice that instructed him to preserve the French capital for future generations, influenced perhaps by the terrible suffering and destruction he had witnessed in the battle for Normandy before taking command in Paris on 8 August 1944. His decision was endorsed by the Swedish Consul General in Paris. Much later his son Timor said: 'France officially refuses to this day to accept it and insists that the Resistance liberated Paris with 2,000 guns against the German army. To official France, my father was swine but every educated French person knows what he did for them. I am very proud of his memory.' It should be noted, however, that when General Choltitz died after a long illness in November 1966, several high-ranking French military officers attended his funeral.

Hitler Digs In His Heels

Any hopes among senior commanders on both sides that Hitler would sue for peace were shattered at a conference held on 31 August. The Führer held forth: 'The time hasn't come for a political decision . . . It is childish and naïve to expect that at a moment of grave military defeats the moment for favourable political dealings has come. Such moments come when you are having successes . . .

'But the time will come when the tension between the Allies will become so great that the break will occur. All the coalitions in history have disintegrated sooner or later.'

In some ways he was right, but the break he depended upon would occur many months after Hitler's death and the destruction of Germany.

On the same occasion he accused the army's general staff of weakening combat officers with pessimism instead of exuding iron will. 'Under all circumstances we will continue this battle until, as Frederick the Great said, one of our damned enemies gets too tired to fight any more. We'll fight until we get a peace which secures the life of the German nation for the next fifty or hundred years and which, above all, does not besmirch our honour a second time as happened in 1918.'

By now the sight of Hitler was but a memory to the German people. Even the sound of his voice was a thing of the past. But his words and his will were transmitted expertly through the offices of propaganda chief Goebbels.

Two days prior to the liberation of Paris, Rumania switched sides after its pro-German premier Ion Antonescu was deposed and replaced with a moderate. King Michael I accepted Moscow's demands for an unconditional surrender while permitting German soldiers to leave without harassment. This was a significant loss for Hitler as with Rumania went substantial oil reserves. Bulgaria had already withdrawn from the Axis, the collective name for the international powers supporting Hitler.

CHAPTER SEVEN

The Low Countries

'I think, sir, that we may be going a bridge too far'

Lieutenant General Sir Frederick Browning, on the plan for Operation Market Garden

Having lost the battle for France, Germany now had to defend occupied territories in the Low Countries and Germany itself. The first German city to fall was Aachen, although its capitulation was a long, drawn-out affair. Troops from the First US Army were in the neighbourhood from 12 September. However, city defenders put up a staunch battle, often inspired by the sight of a swinging corpse from a tree – the punishment meted out by fanatics to those deemed insufficiently loyal to Hitler. It wasn't until 16 October that the city was enveloped by US soldiers and it was a further five days before surrender. It was a milestone that came with a high price tag; 8,000 casualties and five weeks lost. British and Canadian troops were also facing unexpected losses as they mopped up surprisingly fierce opposition along the Channel ports, most of which were savagely destroyed by Germans who had been ordered to stay and fight to the last man. Both British and American forces were being reined in for lack of fuel.

There was friction once again between Allied commanders about the best way to proceed from France into Germany. Eisenhower favoured a broad sweep while Montgomery wanted a sudden drive into Germany to part the Reich from its industrial heartland and so bring the war to an end. In doing so the launch site for the V1 and V2 rockets would be overcome, saving London and the home counties from further destruction.

One British commander, Lieutenant-General Brian Horrocks, had charged ahead into Belgium, bypassing many enemy troops but stopped short of closing the pocket through lack of supplies. Montgomery – who had recently handed the job of commander in chief of land forces to Eisenhower, as Americans would not tolerate a different nationality in charge of US forces – was inspired by this partial success. He considered plans for an operation to capture and secure a Rhine crossing at the Dutch town of Arnhem and elsewhere, to feed Allied armies into the Ruhr, as well as four other vital canal and river bridges. It was called Operation *Comet*. Unfortunately, airborne operations are by their very nature always weather-dependent and *Comet* was twice postponed then finally cancelled on 10 September.

On the same day following a face-to-face meeting Eisenhower was talked into permitting an enlarged operation, diverting some supplies from the Americans

further down France and releasing paratroopers from the First Allied Airborne Army, already put on operational readiness numerous times but stood down as events overtook their planned missions.

To Take The Bridges

With some haste Lieutenant General Frederick Browning and Lieutenant General Dempsey authored a grand plan to supersede *Comet*. Ultimately, the shortage of planning time led commanders to believe the plan should not be changed whatever its flaws. It was to be the largest airborne invasion in history. Yet one of its most significant differences to the smaller-scale *Comet* was the fact that paratroopers destined for Arnhem would now be dropped eight miles from the target bridge rather than by it, as RAF commanders sought to lessen the threat of flak from anti-aircraft guns around the town.

Troopers from the 101st US Airborne division were to grab two bridges at Eindhoven while the 82nd US Airborne division was assigned the task of controlling the waterways at Nijmegen.

German refugees
18 October 1944: German civilians board a US lorry in Aachen bound for a Belgian refugee camp to escape the battle for the city between German and American forces.

Advance with Caution

September 1944: Sergeants J Whawell and J Turrell of the Glider Pilot Regiment of the 1st Allied Airborne Army search a bomb damaged school in the Netherlands for snipers during the Battle of Arnhem.

As Montgomery saw it, there would be a carpet of invaders descending to earth. One wave was to be followed by another while Polish paratroopers were scheduled to drop two days later in the operation. Horrocks would provide the infantry to back up the paratroopers after making a dash through Belgium. If all went well, a salient would be created that would be a corridor into the heart of Holland and on into Germany itself.

It meant the resurrection of the Red Ball Express, the affectionate name for the truck convoys that moved on a one way highway to supply invasion troops in Normandy between 25 August and 6 September. This time it operated between Bayeux and Brussels.

On 17 September the operation began and the paras of the 101st division quickly secured bridges over the Wilhelmina and Zuiter Willemsvaart canals.

From there things went downhill however as the men from the 82nd division captured a single bridge over the Meuse but failed to secure one at Nijmegen in the face of a stout German counter attack. Determined Germans even sent swimmers in the river armed with special charges to blow the bridge, although the attempt amounted to little.

A Bridge Too Far

At Arnhem the remnants of two highly trained SS Panzer division, co-incidentally in the area for a re-fit and recently trained in techniques to repel airborne invasions, were waiting to greet British paratroopers. Dutch resistance intelligence stating as much had been overlooked in the hurry to get the operation underway.

In fact, the element of surprise was lost on two counts. Paratroopers were dropped at two venues – Renkum and Ginkel Heide – up to eight miles from Arnhem and had to trek on foot to the positions they were scheduled to take. Equipment that would have shortened their trip was lost in the drop. At any rate, Germans were well aware of their presence before the red berets appeared at Arnhem.

Also, an American soldier in possession of a copy of the plans for Operation *Market Garden* was captured and the aims of the Allied troops were quickly dispersed among the defenders in Arnhem and its environs. Despite those twin catastrophes the men did capture the north end of one bridge at Arnhem and held it for six days.

The British XXX Corps intention to relieve the paratroopers was continually held up by unexpectedly fierce German opposition. There was more bad weather to contend with also. It left the men aiming to hold the bridges in a precarious position, unable to break down German defences. Polish paratroopers arriving five days after the initial attack were also kept away from the British at Arnhem by determined German fighters.

Among those parachuted into Arnhem on 17 September was Dunkirk veteran Ted Shaw, an officer with the 1st Airborne, whose task it was to support the 3rd Battalion with anti-tank guns:

'Within about quarter of an hour of landing we came to a crossroads. Two German armoured vehicles came along and simply let go with their machine guns. The infantry from the 3rd Battalion went to ground but the driver took a chest full of bullets and died. I had to commandeer a jeep, hitch up the gun and set off again. You didn't get time to worry about the

Digging In

Men of the 1st Paratroop Battalion take cover in a shell hole during the battle for Arnhem, September 1944.

dead. You knew the medics were coming behind. If you started to think about it too deeply nothing else happens. I was responsible not only for my own chaps but for the company ahead. We pushed on with more skirmishes along the way. '

He witnessed the glider arrival of the Polish Parachute Brigade on 19 September under heavy fire that killed many before they touched the ground.

When a company major asked Shaw to use his gun to silence a German ack-ack weapon that was causing havoc for the airborne troops, Shaw replied he only had armour piercing shells rather than high explosives that were needed for the job. Still the major insisted the German gun fire was seriously denting morale. Shaw got the gun into action and fired, silencing the German gun forever.

'But we had a saying among the anti tank gunners that you should never open fire until you see the whites of their eyes.

For once you have fired the enemy knows where you are by the flash of the gun. Afterwards we took terrific casualties because the Germans knew where we were.'

Eventually Shaw lost all four guns he was in charge of but began operating others in Oosterbeek after meeting paratroopers holed up in and around the old church. He saw most of his fellow gunners killed but his actions were recorded in a citation that marks his bravery.

'On the afternoon of 20 September 1944 at Arnhem his gun positions in support of 1st Paratroop Brigade were heavily attacked by enemy tanks and infantry. During that afternoon Lieutenant Shaw gave an almost superhuman display of persistent gallantry.

'His gun detachments were almost all killed or wounded but he himself continued to man a gun until his last companion was killed. On at least three occasions that afternoon he returned to one or other of the guns and manned them with a single companion only leaving them on each occasion when his assistants had all been killed. Lt Shaw's heroism on this most difficult occasion continued for several hours. His consistent and utter disregard of all considerations of personal safety was quite exceptional.'

Ultimately he was awarded a Military Cross rather than the Distinguished Service Order for which he had been recommended in a form countersigned by General Urquhart.

Five nights later he remained in charge of 'walking wounded' housed in a basement in Oosterbeek. When he heard quiet footsteps in the middle of the night he feared they belonged to German soldiers and hushed the injured men. The next morning he emerged at day break to find that all the uninjured British soldiers had disappeared.

He put up a white sheet at the basement where the injured men lay to indicate their surrender then tried to make an escape. His aim was to hide in a wooded area during the day and swim across the Rhine to safety under cover of darkness:

'I could see a copse ahead. I slipped into a stream and waded waist deep in water, tar and muck to get to it. I was just climbing out the other side when I heard the words: "Kommen Sie her'. It was an SS machine gunner. He spoke very good English. He was a bit annoyed at first because I had quite a lot of grenades in pouches on my chest. He took them from me and said: "Two elite divisions and we have won!" I didn't argue with him as I was so vulnerable. When he searched me he found Donald, a paratrooper duck made out of an old army blanket with a beret and medals. "Talisman?" he asked. When I said yes he gave it back to me and I still have it today. But I also had 90 condoms on me, a pack of three for each of the 30 men in my troop. He didn't give those back to me.'

Within nine days all the Allies at Arnhem were compelled to withdraw, leaving some 7,800 men either dead, wounded or prisoner. The operation was a disaster and Montgomery no longer sought for short cuts to end the war. It fulfilled Browning's prediction, that it was 'a bridge too far'. A Hollywood film of the story was made with the same name.

The operation has since been dubbed 'a tragedy of errors' by many of the veterans.

One British soldier in the 1st Parachute Brigade recalls being taken prisoner during the Arnhem operation:

'We were stripped of all our possessions. One of the lads had his wallet taken and a picture of his wife torn up. When he made a move to protest he was shot where he stood. Among the group was a teenage resistance worker who we had begged to get into army uniform in case he was caught but he stood there proudly wearing his orange armband. The German came up to him and said one word – terrorist – and shot this brave youngster through the head. His blood spilt all over me.'

Lance Corporal Slawomir Kwiatkowski of the 1st Polish Independent Parachute Brigade Company dropped into Holland on 21 September:

'I was with a group of Poles who took over the defence of five houses in the Eastern perimeter of Oosterbeek from the British. We stayed there till night from 25 to 26 September. At night the British Airborne Division began to withdraw for evacuation upon the riverbank. There was a distinct shortage of motor boats available and the evacuation proceeded at a very slow pace. It occurred in 'no man's land' in an area called 'the killing ground' because it was covered by German fire. The Poles were the far rearguard and our group arrived almost at the break of day. We saw the row of soldiers waiting and eventually there were no more boats to cross. Then a white flag came out and with the rest of the waiting men I became a prisoner. I was a poor swimmer. From more than 300 Poles fighting in Oosterbeek only 160 crossed back.

The fighting was equally torrid for German soldiers, as Lieutenant Erwin Heck explains:

'Suddenly we found ourselves surrounded by British forces. The fighting was terrible and the closer we got to Oosterbeek the harder the fighting became. Advance became difficult because of the wooded terrain. Once arriving at Oosterbeek we fought man to man, house to house and on

some occasions we occupied one floor of a house and the enemy another. On many occasions we just had to fight with pistols because of this man to man situation. We did not get any rest.'

One of the tragic side effects of Operation *Market Garden* was the suffering of the Dutch people. To assist the Allies the Dutch government-in-exile had called for a general strike before the action took place to hinder the Germans defensive efforts, knowing that severe punishment from the Germans was certain.

German Revenge

About 450 Dutch people perished during the operation, some of whom put themselves in the line of fire by fighting alongside the Allied troops. Others risked their necks by helping the wounded.

Afterwards the Germans punished the Dutch in the immediate area by evicting them from their homes (which had

Crossing the Rhine
US infantrymen huddle down closely on top of each other in an assault boat under heavy enemy fire during the crossing of the Rhine into Germany at St. Goar.

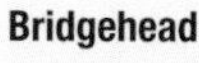

Bridgehead

Allied tanks cross the bridge over the Rhine at Nijmegen, Holland, in the early hours of 21 September, 1944.

already been comprehensively damaged during *Market Garden*.) Their belongings were then looted on behalf of German families living in the bombed-out Ruhr region. Now the Germans aimed to build a defensive line along the north river bank in case of a future attacks.

Then the wider Dutch population under occupation in northern Holland was kept perilously short of food. It was dubbed the 'Hunger Winter' as freezing temperatures and a lack of fuel exacerbated an appalling situation. An estimated 18,000 people died before liberation came to that part of Holland in April 1945.

Nevertheless, the Dutch people continued to assist paratroopers during that bleak winter. While the majority who did not make the retreat were wounded or taken prisoner there was a sizeable minority numbering in the hundreds who had evaded capture and were now living furtively, dependent on Dutch families for their survival. Several large scale operations were organised between the British and Dutch to get the evaders back behind Allied lines. On 22 October about 120 men crossed the Rhine at Renkum although another attempt the following month ended in disarray when it was rumbled by the Germans. Smaller operations continued throughout the winter after it became clear there was going to be no attempt to invade Holland prior to spring.

Market Garden was essentially a seriously flawed plan that was unlikely to succeed. Nevertheless it became a focus of national pride thanks to the astonishing bravery of men fighting against all odds. Afterwards five men were awarded the Victoria Cross, Britain most prestigious gallantry medal.

The Siegfried Line
Soldiers of the US 9th Infantry hitch a lift aboard a Sherman as they cross the tank traps of the Siegfried Line, Germany.

Securing Belgium

Despite *Market Garden*, the Allies continued to edge German soldiers into retreat although it was a protracted process. As a consequence of the resources thrown at *Market Garden* the plan to clear the Scheldt estuary of German resistance was compromised. The prize here was Antwerp, a sea-going port that would solve the growing dilemma surrounding supplies for the Allies. But the land was flat, featureless and frequently flooded by the enemy. When land-based attacks came to nought the Allies resorted to amphibious invasions at two points, Westkapelle and Flushing, going head to head with formidable fortifications. Although the attacks were ultimately successful the Germans fought with ferocity to protect the strategic stronghold. Indeed German resistance was still proving problematic throughout the region.

German Resistance

There was even an unexpected German counter attack at Meijel, near Eindhoven, on 26 October, swiftly countered by men under Dempsey's command.

On 26 November Antwerp, a deep-water port able to supply the advancing Allied armies, was finally open for business. It was an early birthday present for Winston Churchill, who celebrated being 70 just four days later. The triumph of the

Allies was tempered when it became a target for Hitler's retaliation weapon. There were 924 V2 strikes against Antwerp in addition to a further 1,000 by V1 rockets, sinking 60 ships and causing 15,000 casualties, many of them civilian.

US troops pursuing Eisenhower's favoured fan-like attack on Germany reached the West Wall or Siegfried Line, as it was better known to both sides. The Wall ran for 300 miles (480 km) from Basle to Cleves, partly in parallel with the French Maginot Line. Building work had begun in 1936 and it was a major pre-war project in Germany when in one year alone 500,000 people and one third of the country's annual output of cement were used in its construction. It included pillboxes and anti-tank defences that thwarted, but did not entirely halt, the progress of the invaders.

However, fuel shortages did anchor the Allied charge into Germany, permitting the Germans valuable time to regroup. Supplies simply could not be off loaded quickly enough at the freed ports. Also, German forces dogged the progress of the Allies almost every step of the way. Soldiers continued to die throughout the Autumn of 1944 during the push to the Siegfried Line and into the Low Countries. One of the victims was Sgt Major Evan Davies of the 3rd Battalion The Monmouthshire Regiment who was killed by German fire in the Dutch town of Broekhuizen on 30 November. His body was not recovered for nearly 60 years until builders began excavating the site of a housing development. His cap badge, rank insignia and dog tag helped to identify him. His widow Grace said: 'I was told he was missing, presumed dead. I've often wondered and worried what happened to him'. Although she married again she never forgot her first love. He has since been re-buried in Venray Commonwealth War Graves Cemetery in Holland. A Nazi flag seized by his platoon at Helmond in Holland and signed by him two months before his death is on display in the South Wales Borderers Museum in Brecon.

CHAPTER EIGHT

Battle of the Bulge

On being requested to surrender at Bastogne, US Brigadier-General Anthony McAuliffe responded laconically: "Nuts!"

Although German forces were essentially reeling – there was a shortage of manpower, tanks and fuel – a counter-punch still haunted the mind of the Führer and he formulated a plan of attack in the challenging terrain of the Ardennes. 'This will be the great blow which must succeed,' he told his armaments minister Albert Speer. Hitler was cheered by Speer's reports that production of planes and assault guns was rising as slave labourers enduring appalling conditions worked ever harder. He closed his ears to the news the transport links to bring armaments forward were failing badly. Futile though Hitler's dreams were, the alternative was the swift end of the Reich and accordingly he drew on the reluctant support of the weary Wehrmacht generals.

He ordered that this great blow should come in the thick of winter in the forested Ardennes region where it was believed American forces were lax due to spearheads being forged to the north and south. He closed his ears to the plaintiff objections of the generals, that there were insufficient numbers in the attacking force, that the Luftwaffe was impotent, that those men who could be called on were battle weary. His aim was to reach back to Antwerp to stifle Allied activity in the region, close the supply lines and capture numerous prisoners. His best weapon, he knew, was that of tactical surprise. His orders were that ahead of his soldiers there should be 'a wave of terror and fright and that no human inhibitions should be shown.'

Hitler called to the task SS General Sepp Dietrich, a man he labelled as 'simultaneously cunning, energetic and brutal'. Later Dietrich commented with irony about the task given him. 'All I had to do was cross the Meuse, capture Brussels then go on and take Antwerp. All this through the Ardennes where snow was waist deep and there wasn't room for four tanks abreast, let alone six armoured divisions.' Dietrich did voice his apprehensions but was told by Hitler that he would have all he needed at his disposal to make the plan work.

Assembled in secrecy were 30 divisions containing some half million troops in the Sixth SS Panzer Army under Dietrich, the Fifth Panzers under Hasso von Manteuffel and the Seventh Army under Brandenberger with some 1,000 aircraft primed to burst through American lines and split the Allied armies. Morale was high as they sensed the possibility of a mil-

Battle of the Bulge

The attempted breakthrough by Panzer armies in the Ardennes area of France was Hitler's last desperate gamble to stave off defeat by the Allies. It failed.

itary coup while the skull and crossbones insignia of the SS fluttered on flags blown by an icy wind.

The Panzer Armies Attack

Allied commanders simply didn't see the offensive coming. Reconaissance flights were grounded due to bad weather so at least one early warning system was out of action. While code-breakers back in Britain had detected the massing of German troops it was generally thought these would be for an attack when Allies penetrated more deeply into the Reich. Strict radio silence had eliminated the opportunities for eavesdroppers to pick up tell-tale signals.

At first the German fight back seemed little more than an isolated pocket of resistance. General Eisenhower was attending a wedding when the fighting started on 16 December while Montgomery was playing golf. Other Allied commanders were perhaps distracted by news of the death of popular US band leader Glenn Miller, whose plane disappeared over the English Channel.

Holes in the Snow

American soldiers dig hasty foxholes in snow-covered terrain as enemy artillery fire opens up near Berismenil, Belgium. Ardennes campaign, December 1944.

A bid to speed the advance with the drop of paratroopers was not overtly successful as they were scattered over a wide area with few tools of destruction at hand. There were some seeds of confusion sown by German commandos led by Austrian commando Otto Skorzeny – the man who had audaciously rescued Mussolini by glider from captivity in Italy in 1943 – wearing American uniforms driving US vehicles but their effect was for the most part insignificant. It was the sheer astonishment at a German strike that caused maximum chaos among the Americans, unprepared as they were for action.

Fortunately Eisenhower swiftly bolstered the thin US front line by halting other Allied activity in the region and diverting extra troops to where they were most needed. But his foresight was not sufficient to stop a surge by the Germans into territory previously held by the Allies. The Americans were in disarray as German forces sprang up in their vicinity as if from nowhere. A disorganised charge for Allied lines was reminiscent of the German action at Falaise. A few made the most of the Ardennes hills to fire down on advancing Germans while the majority made off before being killed or taken prisoner, hampered by thick mud or snow, lack of food and, later, sleep deprivation. (The biggest failure, of course, lay not among the men but in the inadequacy of intelligence that would have flagged up the gathering German forces.)

There was uncharacteristic chaos too among German soldiers that slowed their advance. One of their biggest problems was a traffic jam that prevented them from making progress to the tight timetable Hitler had in mind. The Ardennes offensive is often called the Battle of the Bulge to reflect the balloon shape it made in the front line.

Among the initial casualties in the bulge were two regiments of the 106th division of the First US Army which were forced to surrender. Indeed, the loss of 7,000 soldiers to imprisonment was one of the greatest hammer blows to the US during the entire conflict. However, a garrison mostly made up of US 101st Airborne troops at Bastogne held out, despite shortages in food and ammunition. When asked by the surrounding Germans to surrender, commander Brigadier General Anthony McAuliffe replied in one word: 'Nuts!'. Bastogne would become the rock that split the German advance.

The Malmedy Massacre

The horrors of war came to haunt Allied soldiers when men from Battery B of the 285th Field Artillery observation Battalion were cut down in cold blood on 17 December by an SS Panzer group from the elite *Leibstandarte Adolf Hitler* led by Colonel Joachim Peiper. The atrocity occurred at the Baugnez crossroads near Malmedy in Belgium after the American men got lost on their way to St Vith.

When a passing Panzer unit blew up the lead American jeep the frightened soldiers readily surrendered their weapons and gave themselves up. (Some were already dead and injured from the brief spate of firing while a few others made an immediate escape.) The remainder were rounded up in a snowy field alongside 11 other American prisoners already captured by the same unit and the military policeman who had been on traffic duty on the crossroads and put under a guard. Already some men felt the chilling air of menace that filled the air. Shortly afterwards Peiper shot off in a tank, shouting at the captured men: 'See you in Tipperary, boys.'

Finally a Rumanian-born private called George Fleps disembarked from an armoured vehicle, strutted about among the Americans and used his Luger pistol to fell two of them. Then automatic weapons on the armoured trucks burst into life, flooring the unarmed Americans.

Following sustained fire which last perhaps three minutes individual German soldiers strolled around the bloodied bodies dispatching the injured with a single shot or the butt of a rifle. Those who tried to make a run for cover were mown down in an instant. The death toll was 100 dead and 41 injured, some of whom were found by American patrols in the area. The same German soldiers were believed to be responsible for the killings of more than 100 Belgian civilians at around the same time. Within a few days the Peiper's spearhead had been brought to a halt by lack of fuel. Word of the massacre whistled around the American lines, causing many men preparing to surrender to have second thoughts. It also resulted in the cold blooded shootings of numerous SS paratroopers who afterwards fell into American hands.

Testimony

Before long, two journalists from *Time* magazine were in the vicinity and spoke to 2nd Lieutenant Virgil Lary, a survivor who had to take dismembered toes and bullets from his boot:

'We didn't stand a goddamned chance . . . We just didn't have a chance.'

The massacre made headlines across the free world and hardened the attitudes of GIs fighting their way across Germany.

Later Lary testified in the postwar trial of Peiper, his superior Sepp Dietrich and other men in the unit which took place at Dachau, the former concentration camp, in 1946:

'After the first machine guns fired men fell dead and wounded all around me . . . A man came by me as I lay feigning death and I heard a pistol shot nearby. Then I heard the sound of a new clip being inserted in a pistol and the individual passed me. I heard someone say to someone else: "Have they killed you yet?" He replied: "No, not yet . . . but if the bastards are going to kill me I wish they would come back and get it over with." A bullet had severed my toes and I was in extreme pain and frozen from head to foot.

'Here and there I heard more raised voices: "Have they gone?" "What shall we do?" "Is it safe?" "Shall we make a run for it?" Suddenly about fifteen of us decided to make a break for it. We had moved a few yards when rifles cracked then a machine gun. I managed to clamber over a fence into a wood and ran along a dirt road until I came to a tumbledown shed. There were bundles of sticks inside and I pulled these all over myself. I waited.'

The chief prosecutor, Lieutenant Colonel Burton Ellis said: 'The troops of the *Leibstandarte Adolf Hitler* were told to excel in the killing of prisoners-of-war as in fighting. Others were told to make plenty of *rabbatz,* which in SS parlance means to have plenty of fun killing everything that comes in sight. Each defendant was a cog in a giant slaughter machine.'

Hidden Danger

Engineers of the 75th Division, Company C, 275th Engineers, sweep a snow covered road for enemy mines.

Although the Germans suggested that the killings occurred after an escape attempt and that plenty of prisoners were taken by the unit in action, proving that there were no broad brush orders to kill prisoners of war, Dietrich, Peiper and 42 others were sentenced to death by the court. The treatment handed out to the Americans at Malmedy was frequently dished out to Russian soldiers on the Eastern front.

However, when evidence emerged suggesting that confessions had been obtained using methods borrowed from the Gestapo, the sentences were commuted to life imprisonment. Peiper was released along with Dietrich in 1958.

The bodies of the dead were not recovered until the middle of January when Americans re-took the region. Even then they were hampered by enemy shelling that might have compromised subsequent examinations of the corpses. A later report by army doctors who carried out autopsies concluded that 43 bodies had gunshot wounds to the head, three suffered severe blows to the head and nine still had their arms raised above their heads.

Massacre at Malmedy

The bodies of murdered American prisoners-of-war lie where they have fallen in the snowy fields around Malmedy, France. The massacre was perpetrated by members of the elite SS Leibstandarte *division.*

Today a memorial with the names of 84 marks the crossroads at Malmedy.

Battling The Weather

The Allied cause during the Battle of the Bulge was hampered by bad weather that kept fighters grounded although many men and numerous tanks were poured into the area in short order. Only when the skies cleared on 22 December did the balance of the battle truly change. The following day Allied aircraft blitzed 31 different targets, badly inhibiting the movement of the panzers and disrupting supply lines. German troop movement was brought to a halt by overhead patrols and a shortage of petrol.

On 27 December a last ditch effort to deprive the Allies of air superiority with the Luftwaffe bombing 27 different airfields foundered: while 156 Allied aircraft were destroyed, a further 300 Luftwaffe planes were shot down.

Eisenhower decided to look upon the attack by the Germans as a opportunity to lasso an unknown number of prisoners and perhaps even shorten the war. His feeling was that the bulge could be made into a bubble and the Germans within it taken out of circulation for the duration of the conflict.

In a report to Congress on the state of the nation given by President Roosevelt on 6 January 1945 the tide of the German fight back was said to be at its height two days after Christmas. 'Since then we have reassumed the offensive, rescued the isolated garrison at Bastogne and forced a German withdrawal along the whole line of the salient.'

To rally a country shaken by the unexpected German counter attack Roosevelt re-iterated: 'Everything we are and have is at stake. Everything we are and have will be given. American men, fighting far from home, have already won victories which the world will never forget. We have no question of the ultimate victory. We have no question of the cost. Our losses will be heavy. We and our Allies will go on fighting together to ultimate total victory.'

Although they were delayed by snow, American army groups organized a pincer action against the Germans and, by the middle of January, the battle was over. Montgomery was given command of two American armies and pitched in to crush the Germans. Later, his words on the subject at a press conference given on 7 January 1945 made it sound like he had mounted a rescue operation and was solely responsible for the victory, when patently the triumph belonged to American soldiers, creating another wedge between British and American generals.

The Consequences of Failure

There were 100,000 German casualties, yet more German soldiers than expected escaped the Americans – probably because they had some considerable experience of fighting in the winter. It was a blow but not a disaster. The movement of troops in the west had stripped the frontier in the east of men and now it proved impossible to hold fast against the Red Army. Enough soldiers were eliminated from the western front to make a difference. Hitler's last ditch effort in the Ardennes had failed – but, although it disrupted embryo plans among the Allies to cross the Rhine, it probably helped to end the war six months earlier than otherwise would have been the case.

Panzer Kaput

One of Germany's last remaining precious Panzers, knocked out by American artillery during the German counter-attack in the Ardennes.

Some German troops were still fighting in Italy, where strategic disagreements among British and American commanders had permitted entire divisions to retreat from Rome to carry out another prolonged campaign of resistance. But the outlook for Germany was bleak.

That fact was starkly evident to many in the Reich. Albert Speer wrote in his memoirs: 'What followed was only the occupation of Germany delayed somewhat by a confused and impotent resistance.' To him it was confused and impotent, but to the men fighting their duty was clear: resistance at all costs, in accordance with the orders of the Führer.

CHAPTER NINE

The Bombing Campaign

'They have sown the wind; let them reap the whirlwind.'

Air Chief Marshal Sir Arthur Harris

Hitler believed he could counter the threat to the Fatherland with the creation of a new people's fighting force, the *Volkssturm*.

On 18 October 1944, following a proclamation by the Führer, the *Volkssturm* was established for all available men aged between 16 and 60, similar in nature to Britain's Home Guard (dissolved less than a month later on 11 November as the threat to the UK was so diminished). Later, as the shortage of soldiers to defend the ever-shrinking Reich became more acute, children as young as ten were invited to arm themselves. Hitler Youth members as young as 12 were among those awarded the Iron Cross by Hitler on his 56th birthday on 20 April 1945 – his final public appearance ten days before his death. Just how the *Volkssturm* would cope against the military wrath of the Allies when the Wehrmacht could not wasn't explained by Hitler. He seemed oblivious of the pathetic sacrifice being made for uncertain reward.

In a speech made on 30 January 1945 celebrating the 12th anniversary of the accession to power of National Socialism in Germany, Hitler made it clear that it was everyone's duty to fight – to the death, if necessary.

Tears of Defeat

Nervous exhaustion is written across the face of a fifteen year old German boy soldier, Hans-Georg Henke, after his capture by the US Ninth Army in Germany.

'He who fights honourably can thus save his own life and the lives on his loved ones. But he who, because of cowardice or lack of character, turns his back on the nation shall inexorably die an ignominious death.'

Amid plenty of references to himself and fellow Germans doing God's work he continued: ' . . .I expect every German to do his duty to the last and that he be willing to take upon himself every sacrifice he will be asked to make; I expect every able-bodied German to fight with the complete disregard for his personal safety; I expect the sick and the weak or those otherwise unavailable for military duty to work with their last strength; I expect city dwellers to forge the weapons for this struggle and I expect the farmer to supply the bread for the soldiers and the workers of this struggle by imposing restrictions upon himself; I expect all women and girls to continue supporting this struggle with utmost fanaticism.'

He went on to call upon German youth to fight 'to safeguard freedom and national honour and thus the future of life'.

Some Germans were heartened by his die-hard attitude – but even they would be brought to their knees by what lay in store for the remnants of the Reich.

The Allied air forces had experimented with area or carpet bombing to some great effect. (In any event, the term precision bombing was something of a misnomer as more bombs flew wide of the target than hit it.) Now Britain's Air Chief Marshal Sir Arthur Harris, commander in chief of British Bomber Command, wanted to obliterate German cities, believing this would lead to a collapse in the national will to wage war. Meanwhile his American counterpart General Carl 'Tooey' Spaatz thought that knocking oil installations out was the key to winning the war. As both pursued their agendas the result was misery for German civilians.

Airfields in Britain, northern France and Italy were available to the Allied air forces and both Britain and America had the capability to fly sorties around the clock. Armaments minister Albert Speer was expecting the onslaught. He was hoping unpredictable Autumn weather would slow down the Allied air campaign sufficiently to keep German production rolling. He was also banking on human frailty playing its part. 'Our one hope is that the other side has an air force General Staff as scatterbrained as ours,' he remarked to Hitler.

Increasing The Pressure

Full scale bombing of Germany began in September 1944 when Eisenhower relinquished first claim on all available aircraft for the purposes of tactical air support during the Normandy campaign. In the next seven months more than 800,000 tons of bombs fell on Germany and thousand-bomber raids became commonplace. The strain of getting into and flying in large formations was as apparent in pilots as the stress of flying in anti-aircraft flak once had been. Germany took some tough punishment, or more specifically, its people did.

One of the prime targets for the Allies was the Leuna chemical fuel works 100 miles south of Berlin. It was bombed on 22 different occasions, reducing its output to on average just nine per cent of its capacity. Fears that the German war machine would be brought to a complete standstill from lack of fuel were looming large. Railway deports, transport yards, factories and industrial heartlands were relentlessly pounded. Slave labourers were those most at risk in these airstrikes, although in bad weather the bombs were dropped without precision, often hitting nearby centres of population.

General Adolf Galland, ace pilot and Luftwaffe commander, planned one final operation against the Allies that would reduce their ability to bomb fuel depots for a while at least, called *der Grosse Schlag* or the Great Blow. He knew it would cost the Luftwaffe dear but felt the losses would be worthwhile if only the capabilities of the enemy airpower were likewise impaired.

Careful housekeeping allowed him to gather together some significant numbers of fighter aircraft. Alas for him, the store was raided in the routine forays against Allied raids as well as Hitler's Ardennes offensive.

Nevertheless, on New Year's Day 1945 The Great Blow was delivered to Allied air bases on the continent in concert with the Battle of the Bulge. Many of the German pilots were dangerously inexperienced while others were hungover from somewhat joyless New Year celebrations. There were far fewer planes in action – some 900 Messerschmitts and Focke-Wulfs – than had been envisaged.

But in their armoury they had the element of surprise and some 206 Allied aircraft were destroyed, most of them still parked up on the ground.

The Allied crews made a swift recovery, however, and pursued the Luftwaffe planes back to Germany. In doing so, 253 Luftwaffe pilots were killed, wounded or taken prisoner. It was a blow from which the Luftwaffe would be unable to recover.

Harris was eager to revert to his policy of bombing centres of population. Sixty years on it is impossible to fathom his reasoning. The British did not collapse under the weight of the Blitz, which tended to unite rather than destroy national will, so there were few grounds to suspect the Germans would.

Harris and some his British commanders barely questioned the morality of bombing women and children although Spaatz did express his concerns. His stance was altered however after the Ardennes offensive after which the pressure to end the war through exhibitions of strength was more acute than ever before. Indeed, retrospective criticism about the timing of the bombing implying that it occurred at the end of the war is misplaced. The Allies were shocked by what happened at Ardennes and Allied soldiers were still perishing on the front line. There was not even the smallest indication of enemy capitulation that might have made the hierarchy hesitate in bombing an internal target. Bombing Berlin had occurred on a regular basis since the Battle of Britain in 1940. An escalation of the campaign, code-named *Thunderclap*, was much debated and delayed until it was largely indiscernible as a separate operation.

The Bombing of Dresden

The most notorious of the air raids was the one against Dresden that took place on 13 and 14 February 1945. This picturesque city with some buildings dating back to the 13th century was swollen with refugees from the east, fleeing Russian troops pressing down from the east.

Dresden was never a priority target for the Allies given that it had little strategic significance – although to imagine it was absorbed only in the manufacture of porcelain china would be naive. But now the war leaders sought tangible evidence of support for the Russians and Dresden had been identified by intelligence as a potential German stronghold. Without doubt Dresden was an important administrative and control centre busy with railway traffic. Certainly, if it were

Firestorm

Miraculously undamaged, statues peer down in disbelief at the destruction of the city of Dresden in the aftermath of the Allied bombing.

bombed it would create confusion among refugees that would itself help to block reinforcements heading east towards the Russians. But the bombing would never have shortened the war.

In Dresden the authorities had been lax about city defences. Rumour was rife that a niece of Churchill's lived in the city and that 'fact' alone would keep it safe from bombers. Germans convinced themselves that 'Florence on the Elbe', as Dresden was known, was the kind of place the Allies would like to establish as a headquarters after the conflict and so would refrain from destroying it. There were no reinforced bomb shelters, except those built by the city burghers. Under the incendiary rain there was no place to hide. The guns which could have defended the city had been moved to the Ruhr.

The first wave of 234 RAF Lancaster bombers hit the city for 17 minutes under cover of darkness. Three hours later, 538 RAF planes arrived, targeting the perimeter of the area already destroyed. In daylight the American Flying Fortresses came, nominally aiming for the city's railway stations and Marshaling yards. The result was firestorms of the kind already experienced in Hamburg. In essence, the numerous fires combined to create one massive ball of flames so the city was turned into an inferno.

Lothar Metzger was nine years old when the attack happened and sought shelter from the bombs with his mother and four sisters.

'The broken remains of our house were burning. On the streets there were burning vehicles and carts with refugees, people, horses, all of them screaming and shouting in fear of death. I saw hurt women, children, old people searching a way through ruins and flames . . . 'We saw terrible things: cremated adults shrunk to the size of small children, pieces of arms and legs, dead people, whole families burnt to death, burning people ran to and fro, burnt coaches filled with civilian refugees, dead rescuers and soldiers, many were calling and looking for their children and families, and fire everywhere, everywhere fire, and all the time the hot wind of the firestorm threw people back into the burning houses they were trying to escape from.'

Ursula Gray, a Dresden resident, recalled how people were pulled into blazing houses by the draughts created in the firestorm. Afterwards, the recovery of bodies was a distressing experience. 'Sometimes a washbasin contained 9 to 10 people because their size had shrunk to a small amount.'

Ultimately, attempts to identify and bury the dead proved futile and mass cremations were organised in the street. No one knows the death toll because the population was inflated perhaps even to double its usual size by refugees. It seems likely, however, that the tally was at least as many as 80,000 and therefore exceeded the total of 71,879 dead following the atom bomb attack on Hiroshima, Japan, later in the year.

Afterwards the Dresden bombing was seized upon by Goebbels and his propaganda ministry, eager to portray it as a slaughter of the innocents. 'They who had lost the ability to weep learned it again at the destruction of Dresden,' said playwright Gerhart Hauptmann. Since then various writers have tried an unlikely balancing act between the evils of the Nazi regime and the death toll at Dresden. The argument about whether or not the bombing of Dresden constituted a war crime that went unpunished will continue. Whatever the rights and wrongs of the operation, 24,800 homes were destroyed and thousands of people died that night. Bomber Harris became known as Butcher Harris, and some crew members on the bombers were tormented by what happened to their life's end.

Bomber Command was frozen out by the Government for its perceived lack of 'fair play'. Harris did not receive a peerage, unlike other high commanders, and Bomber Command remains the only branch of the armed forces without its own campaign medal. It remains a fact, however, that throughout the war, Bomber Command lost 55,000 aircrew, a higher number, as John Keegan has pointed out, than the number of officers killed during the First World War.

CHAPTER TEN

Into the Reich

'Lieb' Vaterland, magst ruhig sein,
Fest steht und treu die Wacht am Rhein!'

(Land of our fathers have no fear
Your watch is true, the line stands here)
Die Wacht am Rhein, *German patriotic song*

Allied bombing slowed down only at the start of April when victory was assured. There was no merit now in wiping out industrial centres and communications networks that would be needed by occupying troops. On 6 April Allied Chiefs of Staff told Bomber Command: 'No great or additional advantage can be expected from attacks on remaining industrial centres, since the full effects would not be likely to mature before hostilities ceased.'

Tactical air support was also of limited value, the risk of bombing Allied soldiers being so high. Now the role of the air forces was to supply soldiers and civilians with food and to transport the wounded or prisoners of war home.

After recovering from the Ardennes offensive the Allies gathered themselves to cross the Rhine. By 9 February the French First Army already wielded control over the left bank of the Upper Rhine. Other Allied forces were choosing their jumping -off points for the invasion of Germany territory. For the Americans the exercise proved much easier than they had at first imagined.

In short order, a detachment of Americans from the 9th Armoured Division, part of the First Army, emerged from the Eifel Woods on the west bank of the Rhine on 7 March to find the Ludendorf railway bridge, near Remagen outside Bonn, and its twin railway lines intact.

Every other bridge along the river had been destroyed by retreating Germans, on the orders of Hitler himself. The Führer had threatened anyone who left a bridge standing with death. He also declared that those who blew up Rhine bridges before German soldiers were safely across would likewise be executed. It left Wehrmacht officers with a tough call on the timing of explosions. Most had, however, detonated their charges and reduced bridges to rubble shortly before the arrival of Allied troops.

That meant that advancing troops had to either wait for sappers to construct a pontoon or for the arrival of personnel carriers. With control of the bridge, however, they could simply march into German territory with ease, at speed.

In charge of the unit, Lieutenant Karl Timmermann led his men towards the bridge only to be greeted by the roar of explosives set by the Germans to destroy the bridge pillars. Somehow the explosions left the bridge intact. US engineers set about defusing another detonator as

The Remagen Bridge

US soldiers cross the Rhine river. Troops of the 9th Armored Division, First US Army, move forward over the bridge at Remagen, Germany to establish a bridgehead in strength on the east bank.

German troops and civilians disappeared into a railway tunnel on the eastern side of the Rhine. It was the same day that Cologne, on the south side of the Ruhr pocket, was occupied by the Allies.

News that the bridge had fallen swiftly to the Americans caused immense excitement at Allied supreme headquarters. Now the order was issued for all soldiers in the vicinity to cross the Rhine at this point. Defence against German counterattacks in the ensuing days was successful. Within 24 hours some 8,000 troops, in addition to tanks and self-propelled guns, made use of it. In reality it was a local triumph and several other crossings needed to be established to facilitate the invasion of Germany. Nevertheless, it proved a useful springboard and a massive psychological boost.

After five divisions made use of it, the bridge collapsed on 17 March, killing 26.

The disaster did little to thwart the Americans who by now had installed several pontoon bridges in the vicinity. However, later inquiries decided the corps commander had not exploited the bridge sufficiently and he was duly dismissed.

Worse awaited the Germans who fled the bridge before it was smashed. Hitler was so enraged when he heard what had happened that he vowed terrible revenge against the Wehrmacht officers who permitted the defensive lapse to occur and in total seven were executed. He turned V-2 rockets on to the site, the only time the weapon was used tactically, but failed to dislodge the Americans.

Albert Speer was filled with dismay at signs of Hitler's ruthlessness. In his memoirs *Inside the Third Reich* he recalls: 'In the Wehrmacht communique of March 18, 1945, I read of the execution of four officers charged with not having blown up the Rhine bridge at Remagen in time. Model had just told me that they were completely innocent. The "shock of Remagen" as it was called kept many of the responsible men in a state of terror until the end of the war.'

The following day Hitler instituted a scorched earth policy in Germany, reasoning that a nation so ungrateful as to lose a war did not deserve the benefit of any infrastructure after the conflict. Speer then went to considerable efforts to secretly countermand the Führer, to save lives and industrial capability for the postwar period.

Across The Rhine

On 22 March Patton's forces made amphibious crossings of the Rhine at Oppenheim, between Mainz and Mannheim. That made two successful American crossings of the river while none had been attempted by the British. Montgomery was about to put that right, however, having carefully cleared the west bank of resistance before forging ahead.

In Operation *Plunder* Montgomery parachuted his men across the Rhine on 23 March out of 2,000 aircraft, with prime minister Winston Churchill a witness of the operation:

Bogged Down

US Sherman tank bogged down in mud during the Ninth Army's drive into the heart of Germany.

'The aircraft faded from sight, and then almost immediately afterwards returned towards us at a different level. The parachutists were invisible even to the best field glasses. But now there was a double murmur and roar of reinforcements arriving and of those who had delivered their attacks returning. Soon one saw with a sense of tragedy aircraft in twos and threes coming back askew, smoking or even in flames. . . . It seemed however that nineteen out of every twenty of the aircraft that had started came back in good order having discharged their mission. This was confirmed by what we heard an hour later when we got back to headquarters . . .

'Things went well all that day. The four assaulting divisions were safely across and established in bridgeheads 5,000 yards deep. The heaviest fighting was at Wesel and Rees. The airborne divisions were going strong and our air operations were most successful.'

Five days after establishing bridgeheads the respective armies broke out into Germany.

Inside the Nazi Camps

If Allied troops assumed their destination was Berlin they were wrong. On 28 March Eisenhower directed his men towards Leipzig, leaving the Russians to take Berlin. With no sign of impending surrender, the numerically superior Allies came to the conclusion they would have to fight through every inch of Germany to secure its defeat.

On their doorsteps the Germans had the Red Army, American and British armies to contend with. Internationally they became a subject of vilification and, during February and March, no fewer than 13 countries declared war on Germany, including Venezuela, Saudi Arabia and Turkey.

Across Germany villages and towns burned as so many European venues had done so in the previous five years of conflict. Some Allied soldiers were hardened in their attitude towards the civilian population after seeing their friends gunned down in action in France. However, the liberation of concentration camps in the

Under Fire

Soldiers of the US 6th Armored Division dodge sniper fire during the capture of Oberdola, Germany.

Reich cast Hitler, his army and his people in a new light. Scenes of despicable carnage and the odour of human suffering stayed with those soldiers who visited the freed camps until the day they died.

GP Robert Hartley Olver was a member of the R Deception Force, a unit charged with misleading the enemy about troop movements and operations. As early as the Battle of El Alamein the deception force was in operation and replica gun emplacements, ammunition dumps and vehicle parks had all been created in Africa out of battlefield debris. Montgomery was impressed with its usefulness and continued to support R Force for the remainder of the war. R Force colonel was David Strangeway, who was given his orders directly by Montgomery, and he had 12 majors and captains ranked beneath him. There were four field companies in R Force charged with transporting inflatable tanks, painted canvases depicting bailey bridges or ammunition and store dumps and road signs. In addition there were signals experts to broadcast bogus troop reports on radio waves or play a soundtrack of busy troop movements to accompany the fake tanks. The devices were used to confuse the enemy both at Pegasus Bridge and in the Bocage.

In April Olver heard by radio that Bergen-Belsen – the concentration camp where Jewish diarist Anne Frank died earlier that year – had been liberated and immediately packed a first aid bag and set out to see if he could help.

'We smelled the stench a mile away and soon found ourselves taking part in the most horrible experience of our lives. The high barbed wire gates were open and just outside we saw a few dozen victims on their stomachs eating the grass and weeds that had survived outside the camp – our first sight of those dreadful striped pyjamas

Atrocity

Emaciated bodies strewn across the ground at Bergen-Belsen concentration camp, liberated by the British in April 1945.

The Beast of Belsen
Commandant of the camp at Bergen-Belsen, Josef Kramer, under British guard after his arrest.

covering virtual skeletons. The main wide road through the camp was thickly strewn with the dead and dying. If the skeleton moved it was still alive. Amongst them were males and females squatting with uncontrollable diarrhoea.

'One of the largest wooden huts lining the main road was the so-called hospital. The dead and dying were so piled up inside that they blocked the windows and jammed the one door. To me the over-riding horror was the fact that the vast proportion of inmates were so far gone that they did not appreciate the fact they were being rescued. To them, one uniform was the same as another.

'As this was the first morning – organised help was just starting – in one area the brutal male guards and foul women in their belts and jackboots were being compelled at bayonet point to collect the dead and carry them to the mass graves. I heard later that some were pushed into the grave to get out as best they could.

'Just inside the gates was an immense neat pile about five feet high and the same wide, stretching for yards composed entirely of boots, shoes and sandals, ripped from the victims and awaiting transport to recycling plants. Most of the females had shaved heads and I found out much later that it all went to be woven into soft shoes for the U-boat crews.

'The excuse given by the odd officer was that the starvation was due to our own forces destroying all communicating roads and rails. They did not realise that we had entered a large new SS training establishment about half a mile away which was filled to bursting with food and medical supplies of all description and also a large fully appointed hospital complete with its staff of doctors and nurses.

'My most poignant memory was to see two little girls aged about four or five, dressed in shabby frocks which were quite clean. Their parents must have sacrificed all for them as they were reasonably nourished.

Arrested

General Karl Veith, commander of the German garrison at Brunswick, is arrested by US troops.

These two were walking along the main road hand in hand, chatting to each other and neatly stepping over limbs and bodies as if they were just having a walk through a stony field.'

As the Royal Army Medical Corps forward hospitals arrived Olver pulled back to his unit. Although he had taken his camera he felt too sick at heart to use it. The nearest he could get to retribution was reducing a wooden eagle and swastika on a hostel in Germany to matchwood.

It is estimated the British found 10,000 unburied bodies, mass graves containing a further 40,000 bodies and 38,500 people barely alive. Of these, about 28,000 died soon afterwards despite the efforts of the medics.

At Belsen and other concentration camps local people were forced to visit and witness the abject cruelty that had gone on in their name. Some protested their ignorance while others surely knew at least something of what occurred behind the barbed wire.

Pacifist Ron Tansley with the Friends Ambulance Unit was charged with clearing the Neuengamme concentration camp and found a local priest to recruit 100 helpers from among the townspeople.

'I told him: "I'm surprised that you, a man of God, could allow the events at the camp to happen." He turned up his sleeve and there was a concentration camp number tattooed on his arm. He had spoken out against it and a few days later he was inside the gates himself. Then he turned to me and asked: "What would you have done?" I have often through about that since.'

It was thankfully a different story for the vast majority of Allied prisoners. Lt. Ted Shaw, of the 1st Airborne, captured at Arnhem had more reason to fear the RAF than his captors.

He was transported from Holland where he was taken prisoner on 26

September across Germany with others in railway cattle trucks. When RAF planes came over the German guards would dive off the train into the nearest ditch but leave the prisoners stranded, at the mercy of Allied fire.

He finally arrived at Oflag 79, an officers' camp in Brunswick, on 20 October. He was one of 2,430 in the camp representing 15 different nationalities including Palestinian, Cypriot, Polish, Greek and South African. He carried out a survey that revealed 39 per cent of the men were married, 56 per cent were single and the remaining five per cent were of an unknown marital status.

There was a severe shortage of food. In a notebook he recorded the daily rations. Breakfast was Ersatz coffee – that's code for acorns – while for lunch there were three boiled potatoes plus hot water. In the afternoon there was Ersatz tea (without milk) to be followed by soup, made of turnips, barley or other equally humble ingredients. The highlight was the arrival of Red Cross parcels but this didn't happen regularly. During six months 'in the bag' he lost a stone in weight when he was already a lean figure.

But he cannot recall any cruel treatment from the guards, although the execution of 50 escapees from Stalag Luft III occurred just six months previously.

'Every day the Germans would issue a communique in which they were inevitably on top. But we had a secret radio and we knew what was going on. The men from three huts came into one to listen to the communique when really we were listening to the radio. Our own chaps were posted outside in case a German came in. The warning cry was 'goon up'. Eventually they were saying it themselves as they came into the huts, which made us laugh a lot. 'If we knew a chap wanted to make an escape we would mess the guards around terribly when it came to roll call. We were supposed to line up to be counted and we were all over the place.'

Liberation

Prisoners from the officers' prisoner of war camp Oflag 79 after their release.

One incarcerated officer walked out of the camp dressed in workmen's overalls with a toilet seat slung around his neck. However, no escape plan, no matter how audacious, was successful. The escapees were punished with a spell in solitary confinement. For his part Shaw was simply delighted to survive his spell behind barbed wire.

'I have led a charmed life. I have been in trenches behind a gun being heavily shelled and chaps on either side of me have died. You couldn't see a mark on them but their lungs burst with the blast. That happened two or three times. The person that really had it hard was my wife Dorothy. She was pregnant when I left. All the officers except one left their wives pregnant. She received a telegram shortly after I was captured to say I was missing in action. It was weeks that she had confirmation that I was still alive.'

Liberated

On 12 April the prisoners at Oflag 79 awoke to find their guards missing and liberating American forces at the gate. When Ted finally got home he was greeted by two month old daughter Elaine.

The potentially hostile response of guards did put an end to one escape plan hatched at Colditz, the high security prison in Germany holding some of the most active and ambitious escapees. Two pilots, Jack Best and Bill Goldfinch, who were sent there after fleeing another prison, decided to build a two man glider and this time fly to freedom from the Colditz castle roof. The runway was to be made out of tables while the glider would be catapulted on pulleys connected to a bath filled with concrete that would be tossed over the castle wall. Although the glider was completed in October 1999, the fate of those caught after 'the Great Escape' weighed heavily on the minds of its builders. With the end of the war in sight, it seemed an unnecessary risk to take. However, a 1999 replica glider built and launched on the same principles proved the plan would have worked.

The Allied advance continued, challenged but largely unchecked by defending Germans. The huge country was being dissected by Allied spearheads, several of which were aiming to link up with Red Army columns in the east. Others were heading towards Bavaria and Austria to contend with the National Redoubt, or last stand of the Nazis rumoured to be planned for Hitler's retreat at Berchtesgaden. In fact it was a mythical notion. On 1 April Model's Army Group was enveloped in the Ruhr, offering up literally thousands more prisoners. Believing the calamity to be worse than that of Stalingrad in 1943, Model felt so disgraced and despairing that he committed suicide in a wood near Duisburg.

He knew that Germany had not just been overwhelmed but had been outfought. US military naivety was a thing of the past, British tactical clumsiness was now a matter for history while the chaos that once characterised the Soviet forces had been eliminated. Any last hope for the Reich was gone.

The Wehrmacht, however, continued its heroic, doomed resistance. It was usually not for some misplaced loyalty to Hitler or a mindless acceptance of orders from on high. Soldiers rationalised the continuing battles in the belief they were fighting for their families whom they perceived to be in mortal danger.

CHAPTER ELEVEN

The Fall of Berlin

'Whosoever gives you a command to retreat is ... to be arrested immediately and if necessary to be executed immediately, irrespective of his rank.'

Hitler order to the Wehrmacht, 16 April 1945

To mark the 27th anniversary of the Red Army and navy in February 1945, Stalin gave a speech that outlined the progress of Soviet forces.

'Within forty days of the offensive in January-February 1945 our troops ejected the Germans from 300 towns, captured about 100 war plants manufacturing tanks, aircraft, armaments and ammunition, occupied over 2,400 railway stations and seized a network of railways totalling over 15,000 km in length.
Within this short period Germany lost over 350,000 officers and men in war prisoners and not less than 800,000 were killed.
During the same period, the Red Army destroyed or seized about 3,000 German aircraft, over 4,500 tanks and self-propelled guns and not less than 12,000 guns.'

Even allowing for exaggeration the successes of the Red Army were apparent to all. Stalin was speaking just weeks after Soviet soldiers liberated Auschwitz death camp in Poland. They camped in their positions during the worst of the winter weather before beginning a final, inevitable thrust towards the German capital. Yet still Hitler refused to acknowledge the inevitable and contemplate surrender.

The first Germans to suffer the Russia onslaught had been those living in East Prussia, a pint-sized state created after the First World War and willingly under Reich rule. The Russian offensive began on 12 January and was swift. Defence of the region was compromised by Hitler's meddling in military matters. He had switched vital divisions to different parts of Europe without telling his Wehrmacht commanders even after the battle had begun.

Russian troops moved from the Vistula to the Oder between 12 and 31 January. It meant East Prussia was scythed from the Reich and ultimately defenders on the north coast would have their backs to the sea. While enforcing Hitler's 'no surrender' policy for a hapless population, East Prussian Nazis were plotting their own escape.

Fleeing The Red Army

Civilian evacuation was tragically belated and conducted in severe weather conditions. Numerous women and children froze to death as they tried to flee the Russian advance. The refugee backlog clogged up artery roads that were vital to the German forces. It wasn't until 21 January that Grand Admiral Dönitz gave

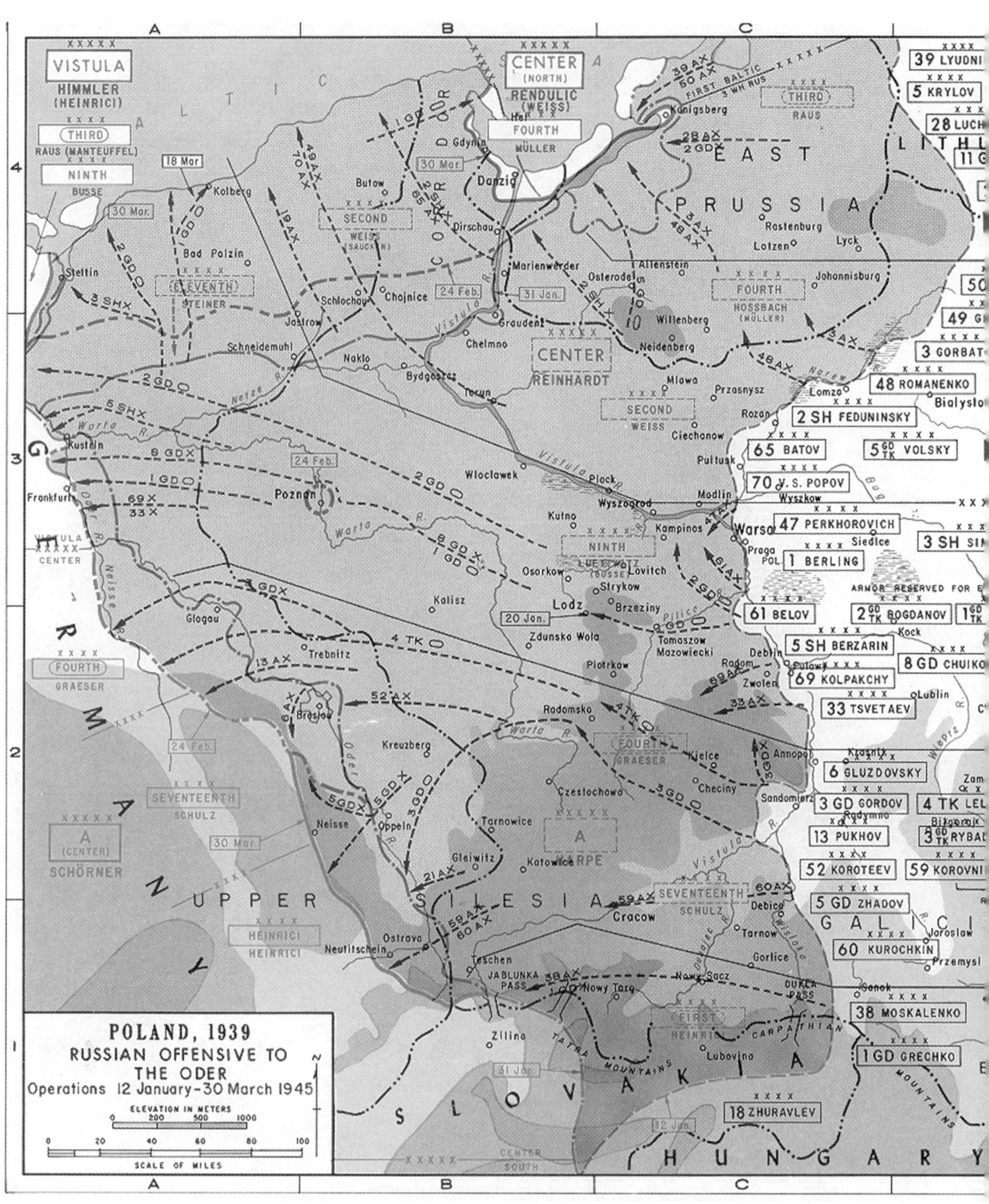

the go ahead for a mass sea-borne evacuation of refugees. Four large ships were designated for the purpose. Nine days later the *Wilhelm Gustloff*, built for 2,000 passengers, set sail from Gdynia with possibly as many as 9,000 aboard. That same night three torpedoes from a Soviet submarine holed the ship, sending it to the

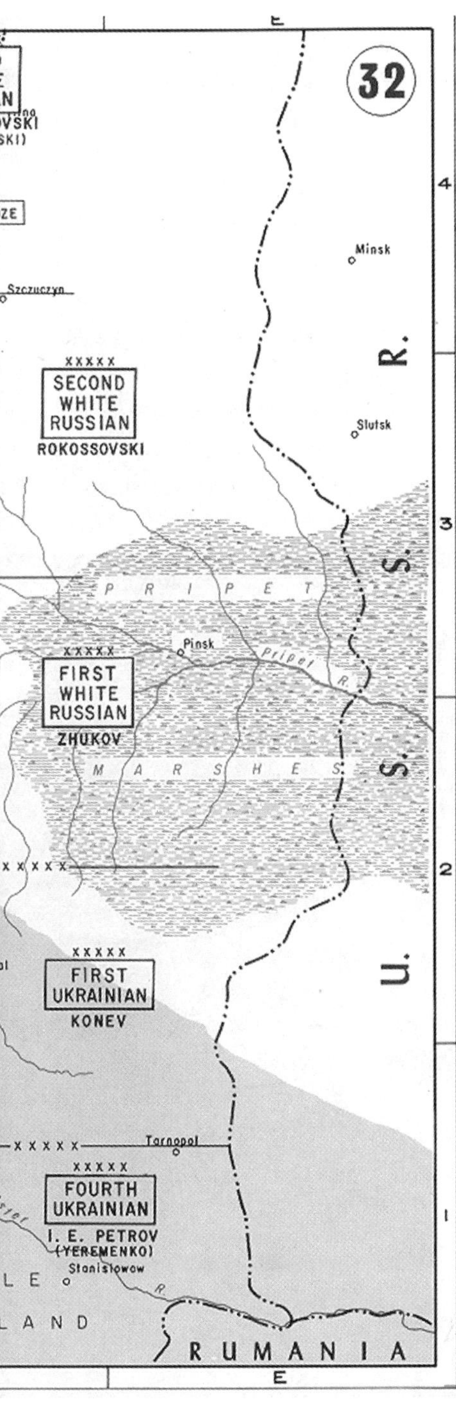

ocean bottom in less than an hour. The scrabbling for lifeboat places probably cost more lives than were saved. Many perished as they floundered in the icy sea, with just 1,300 people being picked up by the nearby cruiser *Admiral Hipper*. It is thought that between 5,300 and 7,400 people died – possibly four times or more the number killed when the *Titanic* sank in 1912.

A Brutal Revenge

Those that remained in East Prussia were at risk from pitiless and often drunken Russian soldiers who sought revenge for the punishment meted out to the civilian population by Germans during their time in Russia. In 1945 the trapped German women knew nothing of the crimes committed by their countrymen a few years previously. Nor were they expecting the outrage felt by most Russians against all Germans that had been carefully cultivated by Stalin. One woman gave an account of her experiences in East Prussia after it had fallen under Russian control:

> *'On 3 February frontline troops of the Red army entered the town. They came into the cellar where we were hiding and pointed their weapons at me and the other two women and ordered us into the yard. In the yard 12 soldiers in turn raped me. Other soldiers did the same to my two neighbours. The following night six drunken soldiers broke into our cellar and raped us in front of the children. On 5 February three soldiers came and on 6 February eight drunken soldiers also raped and beat us.'*

Afterwards she and the other women failed in a suicide attempt for want of a sharpened knife. Alongside the rapes there was looting, arson and wanton violence. The story was repeated wholesale across

Captured
Soldiers of the Red Army round up Volkssturm (Home Guard) troops in the German town of Schneidemuhl (modern Pila in Poland), 1945.

East Prussia, Poland and Germany itself. A monthly five-kilo package home was permitted for Russian soldiers and they crammed it with items plundered from German homes. Hitler's response was to install Heinrich Himmler, a notoriously cruel SS commander with little actual experience in the field, at the head of the battered Prussian armies, believing a stiffer mettle among the commanding officers of the Wehrmacht would alter Germany's fortunes in war.

Yet not all Russians behaved barbarously. There were numerous examples of Red Army soldiers showing kindness, especially to children, even during the height of the horrendous battle for Berlin.

And it was not tales of Russian barbarism but aching hunger that led to a riot in Berlin on 30 January. Some women were openly hostile to uniformed officers.

Hitler's Self-Delusion

Hitler certainly knew the savagery of the fighting in the east. In a speech given on 16 April 1945 he gave a swift pen portrait of life for the Germans being vanquished by the Red Army. 'While old men and children are being murdered, women and girls are humiliated to the status of barracks' prostitutes. Others are marched off to Siberia'.

Yet still he apparently refused to entertain the notion of defeat, especially at the hands of the Russians. Rather than tempering his words with caution or urging civilians to flee to safety he grimly called for greater sacrifice than ever before:

'Whosoever does not do his duty at this moment is a traitor to our nation. The regiment or division that leaves its position acts so disgracefully that it will have to be ashamed before the women and children who are withstanding the bombing terror in our towns.
Above all look out for the treacherous few officers and soldiers who, to secure their own miserable lives, will fights against us in Russian pay, perhaps even in German uniform. Whosoever gives you a command to retreat is, unless you know him well, to be arrested immediately and if necessary to be executed immediately, irrespective of his rank.'

With this man-the-barricades and lay-down-your-lives attitude the Bolshevik menace would drown in a blood bath, Hitler promised. The speech was delivered in the usual strained pitches and high tempo. Apparently only one recording of Hitler speaking in normal tones exists.

These words were an inspiration to some Nazis who freely shot and killed Germans who retreated or contemplated surrender.

If his voice sounded robust then it deceived the listener for Hitler was in poor physical shape. The attempt on his life in July 1944 had accelerated a decline in his health. Now he stooped, dragged one leg when he walked and his left arm shook, sometimes uncontrollably. He was also verging on paranoia and distrusted practically everyone around him, from senior army generals to his doctors.

Perhaps more significant for the fighting men in his charge, Hitler – who in victory had been nimble minded and instinctive – had hit the buffers with regard to military ideas. Following the failure of the Ardennes offensive he was unable to latch on to any meaningful plan of action. Instead, he retreated behind his one long term intensely damaging strategy, which was 'no withdrawal'.

In the last month of his life he grasped slim hope like a drowning man catching hold of a lifeline.

Prisoner of War

The end of the war was within sight, yet still the killing and the dying continued. Jack Goldstein, one of a seven-man crew in a Lancaster Mark I bomber, died on 16 March 1945 during the last air raid over Nuremberg. A mid-upper gunner in 166 squadron based at Kirmington, Lincolnshire, he was the only one from his aircraft who didn't return home after hostilities. Twenty six planes set off that night to pound the significant city of Nuremberg, where Hitler had held so many image-enhancing rallies at the zenith of his power. Subsequent research has revealed that two of the planes crashed in the vicinity of Kammerstein. There were six dead – three Canadians and three English – from one plane, with one man being taken prisoner.

Later, Sgt Goldstein's body was put in a local church with the dead, while his remaining crew members, two from the Royal Canadian Air Force and four from the Royal Air Force volunteer reserves, were captured. The dead were soon buried in a communal grave at nearby Schwabach. In the summer of 1947 his body was exhumed and placed in a cemetery at Durnbach, Bavaria, containing the bodies of some 2,868 Allied casualties, including Indians, South Africans, Norwegians and New Zealanders. It is the most southerly cemetery of its type in Germany, lying just 50 kilometres (40 miles) from the Austrian border. The exhumation report reveals that the 33-year-old Goldstein was buried in his flying suit. Although no distinguishing marks were by then apparent, his identity was established by a process of elimination. His son Michael remembers the arrival of a telegram bearing the bad news.

'I was not yet six when my mother got the telegram. I remember my mother taking it to the light in the scullery. I wanted to know what it was. She said my father was missing. I didn't know what that really meant but she was obviously deeply distressed and asked me to go outside and play. It must have been the worst moment of her life. Afterwards my mother rarely spoke about my father. She grieved inside and wanted to spare the children from hurt.

Initially, fellow crew member Ted Hull believed he saw Jack Goldstein being hauled away to face a firing squad at a prisoner of war camp. Although he was suffering burns and concussion, Hull, a flight engineer, was interrogated three times by a pair of SS officers who accused him of being a Jew from a Jewish

A Final Photo-Op

In his last official photo, Adolf Hitler leaves the safety of his bunker to award decorations to members of Hitler Youth, even as the Russian armies of Zhukov and Konev close in on his final refuge.

squadron. From their words he knew they were aware that Goldstein – who refused to change his name as many had to disguise his religion – was Jewish. Indeed, his dog tag would have indicated his faith. Afterwards Hull was kept in a log cabin about the size of a garden shed. From the window he saw inmates being led to an area he called 'the pits'. 'I was certain one of them was Jack as he was very distinctive'. However, further investigations revealed it was much more likely that Jack died inside the plane. After the pilot gave the order to bale out, one of the departing crew members slapped Goldstein's legs dangling from his gunner's perch in the top of the plane. He received no response. It is almost certain that Goldstein perished when he was hit by fire from an attacking Luftwaffe Ju88. Remarkably, it seems the Lancaster did not explode when it hit the ground, even though it still carried a 4,000 lb bomb in its undercarriage.

Hull was introduced to his future wife by Goldstein and knew him well. But fearful and confused by his injuries, Hull – who felt he heard gunfire when he arrived at the camp and graves being dug – surely mistook another ill-fated prisoner for Jack. Of five brothers serving in the forces during the Second World War Jack was the only one who didn't return. (His brothers were Lou, who served in the Royal Army Service Corps, Mossy, a PT instructor in the King's Royal Rifle Corps, Mick, with the Royal Fusiliers, the Royal Artillery and latterly the Jewish Brigade in Italy, and Ron, a wireless operator who finished the war in the 4th Queen's Own Hussars.) Ron had already celebrated VE Day in Italy believing his family had escaped unscathed when he received a letter to say Jack was missing. Fifty years later he realised he knew little about the circumstances of his brother's death and began painstaking research that pieced the story together. Although he feels his brother died inside the aircraft he knew from his own experience that captured British Jews were at risk of being shot by their captors. This follows a conversation he once had with a German prisoner of war in Austria. Ron's regiment, the 4th Queen's Own Hussars, had set up a Prisoner of War camp at Ferndorf in Austria to accommodate a Cavalry Division which had just surrendered. The Germans were made to be responsible for patrolling the inner perimeter of the cage while the British used to control the outer barbed wire fence. One night Ron struck up a conversation with his German counterpart inside the camp:

'I told him I was Jewish, to which I got the almost automatic response: "Ich habe so viel Freunden Juden!" (I have so many Jewish friends) and I asked him as a matter of academic interest what would have happened if, some weeks earlier, I had the misfortune to be captured by his own unit and they discovered I was Jewish.

He considered the matter for a moment and then told me that if I had been one of a large group of prisoners, then no attempt would have been made to segregate me and I would have just been sent to the rear with the others. If, however, I had been captured separately and if his own officer said to him "shoot him", then he would simply have shot me for, as he quite cheerfully pointed out to me:

"If I don't shoot you then he shoots me!"

At the time it all seemed perfectly logical to both us and I have often been glad that events had never put the matter to the test.'

East Meets West

US soldiers link up with their Russian counterparts on the Elbe, May 1945, splitting Germany from east to west and cutting off Berlin.

The Roosevelt Fallacy

Upon the death of Roosevelt on 12 April 1945 Hitler rejoiced. The world's greatest war criminal was dead, he asserted. He interpreted Truman's inaugural words as being against the European war and in favour only of US action in the Pacific. This led him towards a second fallacy and the idea that the Western powers would join forces with Germany to fend off Russia – something of a hardy chestnut in Hitler's camp – once again had currency as the darkest hour in the bunker approached. A few hopelessly optimistic souls, Hitler among them, believed it could happen.

Against the odds the Grand Alliance, as Churchill described the association of nations that fought the Axis powers, was holding firm. A conference at Yalta in February 1945 had already agreed the principles of a post-war division of Europe. True, there were plenty of grounds remaining for disagreement but these were largely swept under the carpet. The Allied strength of unity would last until after the end of the conflict, when it dramatically dissolved into dust.

On Hitler's 56th birthday on 20 April the celebrations were muted as the Russian artillery guns rumbled in the near distance. Nevertheless, staff and top flight Nazis all proffered greetings laced with familiar expressions of undying loyalty. Hitler marked the occasion by presenting young warriors in the Hitler Youth with bravery medals in the Reich Chancellery Park, under the proud gaze of Reich youth leader Artur Axmann. It was the last time he was outdoors.

Hitler had decided against skipping to the relative safety of Berchtesgaden, his Alpine home, unlike most of his generals and staff who headed there on eleventh hour flights out of Berlin. (Nazi treasures, mostly looted from overrun countries, had been dispatched there a week previously.) He also dismissed the notion that he should die a hero's death, fighting alongside his soldiers, on account of his poor health. But he was insistent that he stayed in Berlin – and that meant staying inside the bunker – and freely spoke about shooting himself, to the consternation of his loyal circle. A day later he had rustled up a defence plan and boasted: 'The Russians will suffer the greatest defeat, the bloodiest defeat in their history before the gates of Berlin.' By contrast, on 22 April, Hitler announced for the first time that there was no hope.

At least some of the mood swings were attributable to drugs and depression but they led to valued advisors lying to Hitler, finding themselves too afraid to tell him an unpalatable truth. He was, by now, ever more free with his threats to execute officers found wanting. He rallied a little when he organised Berlin's final stand, ordering every serviceman to the capital to fight for its survival.

Bizarrely, he displayed a gentler side to his secretaries whom he gathered to dispatch out of the city. 'It's all lost, hopelessly lost,' he told them. After Eva Braun gave an emotional speech about how she would never leave his side the secretaries found themselves also insisting on staying. Shortly before her death, Traudl Junge published a book telling her story. She confessed: 'I was fascinated by Adolf Hitler. He was a pleasant boss and a fatherly friend. I deliberately ignored all the warning voices inside me and enjoyed the time by his side almost until the bitter end.' However, she insisted she knew

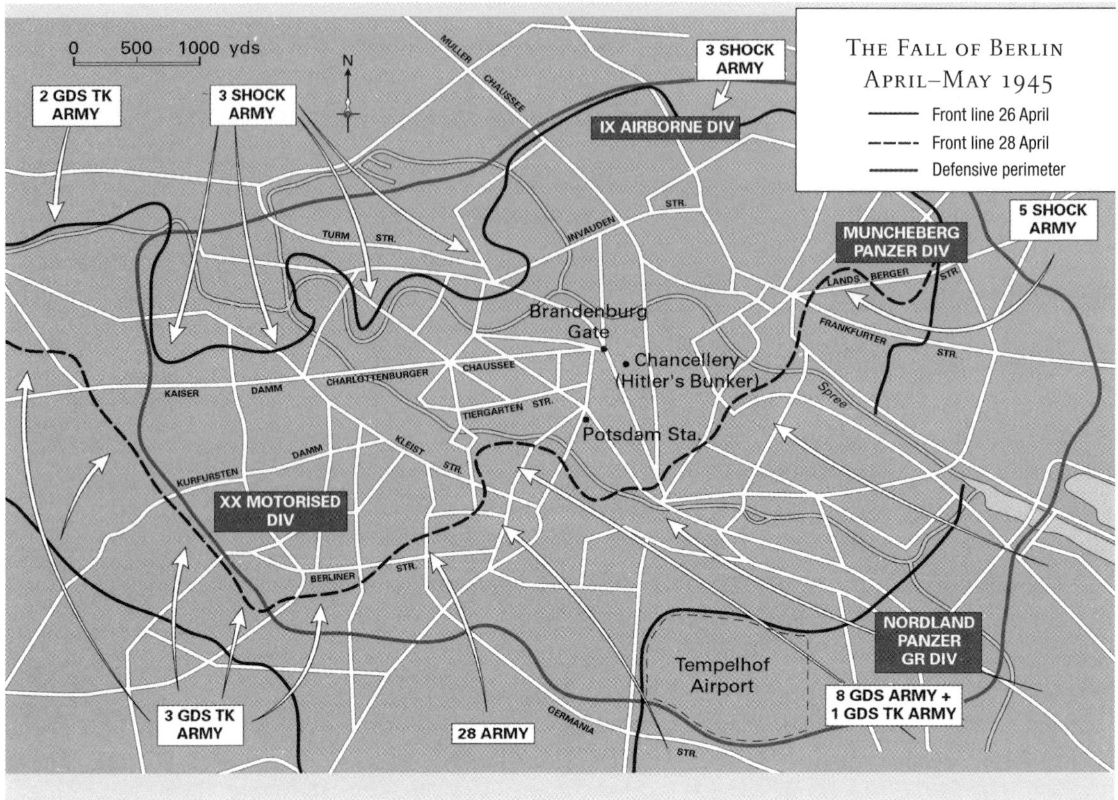

Berlin Under Siege

As Soviet troops under Marshals Konev and Zhukov competed to take the city first, Hitler's Reich shrank to the size of his own bunker.

nothing of mass killings. 'We were in the wings and yet we knew nothing of what was going on the stage. It was only the director who was familiar with the play.'

On 25 April the city centre was under persistent artillery fire although Hitler, facilitated perhaps by his cocaine eye-drops, insisted that things looked worse than they really were. He awaited with anticipation the arrival of an army group he felt would turn the tide of battle. That same day the Berghof, Hitler's beloved home in Bavaria, was smashed by RAF bombers. Miles away from Berlin again American and British soldiers were enjoying a convivial smoke and sup with their Russian counterparts at Torgau.

The battle for Berlin was bitter, raging from street to street, and from house to house. Every time the Red Army soldiers turned into a road they faced a barricade and sniper fire from several storeys above. However, no matter how chaotic it appeared, the Russians were sticking to a carefully constructed plan to encircle the city. Its defenders were mostly reliant on their own initiative.

The End In Sight

With Hitler in a malaise there was a power vacuum that meant no orders were filtered down to the men and boys manning the front line defences in the city. The atmosphere in the bunker was now the south side of gloomy, with the wittiest comment being that it was more morgue than command post and its occupants were the living dead.

Hitler was brought sharply back to reality when his close associates began deserting his cause. He received a telegram from Göring forewarning him that, as Hitler was holed up and impotent in Berlin, the Luftwaffe chief was about to step into his shoes as supremo of the Reich. This was according to a line of succession drawn up by Hitler in 1941. Göring's unspoken agenda was to negotiate an immediate surrender with the Allies. Now Hitler was aghast at what he read. 'To give me an ultimatum,' Hitler marvelled. 'That really is the end.' He punished the treachery by firing off a telegram immediately stripping Göring of his right and placing him under house arrest.

News agency reports that the SS *Reichsführer* Heinrich Himmler, previously an unquestioned lackey, was trying to open peace negotiations with the west were also brought to Hitler. (Martin Bormann had latterly usurped Himmler as the heir apparent during that final month.) Himmler was duly expelled from the party.

On 28 April Benito Mussolini, Hitler's none too effective partner in Italy was captured, tried and executed by partisans in Milan. His body, alongside that of his mistress Clara Petacci, was strung up in central Milan and abused by a mob. Despite the Italian's shortcomings as a military leader, Hitler had obvious affection for him.

Fallen For The Führer
As the 'Thousand-Year Reich' went down in flames, many German officers, such as this general of the Volkssturm, decided their duty lay in taking their own lives.

Devotion Unto Death
Hitler with his faithful companion, Eva Braun, pictured here during happier times at the Berghof. Braun would commit suicide with the dictator as the Red Army closed the ring of steel around Berlin.

Hitler decided to leave his last testimony in the early hours of 29 April and secretary Traudl Junge was filled with nervous anticipation:

'I was going to be the first one to know the explanation of why the war had come to this end, why Hitler could not stop. It was the moment of truth.'

But once again Hitler proved with his own words that he was seriously deluded:

'My heart was thumping when I wrote down what Hitler said but he used nothing new. He came out with these old phrases. He repeated his accusations about the Jewish capitalist system then he announced in the second part of this a new government. It was senseless.'

The political testament contained the following baffling statement: 'It is untrue that I or anybody else in Germany wanted war in 1939. It was desired and instigated exclusively by those international statesmen who were either of Jewish origin or working for Jewish interests. I have made so many offers for the reduction and elimination of armaments, which posterity cannot explain away for all eternity, that the responsibility for the outbreak of this war cannot rest on me.'

He went on to name Admiral Karl Dönitz, the former U boat supremo at that time commander of the German navy, as President of the Reich and Dr Goebbels as the Chancellor.

The same day he married Eva Braun, the faithful mistress, probably at her request. She did so knowing there was no future in the marriage. It was merely a formality prior to death.

Suicide In The Bunker

Eva Braun had requested a painless way to die. She didn't want her death mask to be contorted with agony, she explained to Hitler. The recommendation was cyanide and she and Hitler were furnished with glass vials for the purpose.

Now the very poison which had been supplied by a member of Himmler's office was under scrutiny. Hitler believed it could have been formulated to keep him paralysed but alive and that he would be taken from the bunker against his will. Accordingly, he had some administered to his beloved dog Blondie by way of a test. The loyal Alsatian promptly died.

As the sound of a single shot rang out through the bunker on 30 April remaining staff realised that Hitler and his wife had ended their lives, as both had pledged on numerous occasions to do.

Heinz Linge, Hitler's valet, entered his master's quarters with Martin Bormann and gave the following account of the death of a tyrant:

'Hitler was sitting on the left of the sofa with his face bent slightly forward and

Last Refuge

The Reich Chancellery building, underneath which Hitler had his bunker, burned and bombed out during the final days of the battle for Berlin.

The Dictator's Lair

Russian soldier in the Führerbunker beneath the Reich Chancellery. The sofa visible to the rear is allegedly where Eva Braun committed suicide.

hanging to the right. With the 7.65 (gun) he had shot himself in the right temple. The blood had run down on to the carpet and from this pool of blood a splash had got on to the sofa.'

'Eva Braun was sitting on his right. Eva Braun had drawn both her legs on to the sofa and was sitting there with cramped lips so that it immediately became clear to us that that she had taken cyanide. I took Hitler by his neck, behind me there were two other officers from his bodyguard, and we took Hitler's body and proceeded with it into the park.'

It was now down to Linge to ensure Hitler's orders were carried out, that the bodies were burnt so that no part of them could be held as a trophy by the enemy.

'In the park we laid the bodies together next to each other and poured the available petrol over them. In the Reich Chancellery Park there was fire all around. A draught had got up so we could not set the corpses alight with an ordinary match. So I twisted a taper out of some paper from a notebook and Bormann had come outside with other officers. He lit the taper and I threw it on the bodies and in an instant the corpses were alight.'

It was the end of 12 years and three months of Hitlerite rule. When he came to power there were nine million Jews living throughout Europe. By the time he pulled the trigger two out of every three was dead. The number killed overall during the Second World War is put at 55 million.

Burnt Corpses

Secrecy about the Russian operation to remove Hitler's body caused rumour and speculation about his death. However, subsequent reports have revealed that the bodies of Hitler and Eva Braun were discovered on 4 May. An autopsy found that they were charred beyond recognition, and the extremities were particularly badly burnt. A strong smell of bitter almonds remained, however, leading the senior doctor carrying out the post mortem to believe that cyanide had been used. A piece of the skull on one body was also missing, perhaps because it had been shot away.

The bodies in the mortuary were somewhat shorter than Hitler and Eva Braun were known to be. Shrinkage was almost certainly caused by the intense heat of the cremation.

Two days after the double suicide Berlin surrendered to the Soviet army. Five days later General Alfred Jodl signed the unconditional surrender that ended the European war. (Although Jodl was found guilty of war crimes at the Nuremberg trials and hanged, he was later exonerated by a de-Nazification court in 1953.) There were unbridled celebrations among populations that had learned to live alongside death and disaster.

In Churchill's words:

Hole in the Ground
Russian, British and American officers gaze into the rude grave in the garden of the Reich Chancellery, where the remains of Hitler and Eva Braun were hurriedly interred by the dictator's faithful SS interns.

Surrender

Grand Admiral Karl Dönitz (centre), appointed ruler of Germany in Hitler's final bizarre testament, in British custody. With him are Armaments Minister Albert Speer (l), and General Alfred Jodl, Chief of Staff of the Wehrmacht.

'The unconditional surrender of our enemies was the signal for the greatest outburst of joy in the history of mankind. The vanquished as well as the victors felt inexpressible relief. . . Weary and worn, impoverished but undaunted and now triumphant, we had a moment that was sublime.'

The war had provided spectacles of carnage and chaos, that most everyone wanted to dispatch to history. But the acts of inhumanity were partly weighed by examples of compassion, like the civilian families who risked their lives to shelter wounded soldiers, like the German lieutenant who leapt into action when he heard an American tankman shriek for help in his burning vehicle and tried to save his life, like the soldiers who time after time laid their lives on the line to save their buddies.

VE Day was 9 May, the same day that German forces in Prague gave themselves up to the Red Army. It was as much a relief to the hungry, shattered Germans as it was to the Allies.

Ulla Dellbanco grew up during the war in Germany, the daughter of a Danish teacher with Jewish ancestry. Her mother refused to listen to Hitler on the radio, claiming she could not bear his voice, and she risked her life to listen to the BBC.

'Many distant relations of ours were gassed. We as children knew nothing about it. My father had a good friend in the education office and he put him from one town to another to make it difficult for the authorities to find out about him being Jewish.

When war broke out school was stopped and I was very happy. My brother, who was 12, explained to me what it meant, that soldiers had to shoot others and that houses would be ruined. I said it was a pity that war had come. He said it was a catastrophe. I was in the Hitler Youth. It was obligatory from the age of ten. We had to do some marching but not much and we should have worn a uniform. My sister and I only had one between us and didn't normally wear it. We did a lot of singing and playing and we did entertainment evenings for the soldiers stationed in our town. At Christmas we did not do proper carols but songs about the nation. We were given a book that had in it direct attacks on Jews. I didn't believe it yet I still felt the Jews were not up to standard somehow. It was clever propaganda.'

Today Ulla believes she was for a long time naïve about what was going on in Germany.

'Towards the end of the war my sister and I saw hundreds of concentration camp prisoners. Until then we didn't know such a thing existed. We noticed them from about a kilometre away from the smell. They looked like ghosts, they shuffled along and it was absolutely quiet. No one said a word.

'In the evening they returned with the dead ones over their shoulders. The soldiers were SS armed with rifles. You didn't dare make objections. If anybody had said a word they would have been in the concentration camp the same day. It could cost you your life.'

'The winter of 1944 was very cold. Many people froze. Old people still speak about it because it was so traumatic. My brother Helmut was called into military service on 5 February 1945. After one month's military education he was given a uniform and taken first to Kiel then to Czechoslovakia. He was caught by the Russians and had to spend five years working in the Russian mines.

'For a year we didn't know where he was. We thought about him all the time and I dreamt about him every night. When he came back on the last day of 1949 he was small and thin. The people in the camp were all very kind and he only talked well of them. But it is a wonder he survived. He spent nine months in hospital and had to be re-admitted again after that.

'I don't think anyone ever dared to speak out against the Nazis. I said a prayer every evening and I begged for peace, not for victory. Towards the end I saw it could not be our victory. Hitler claimed he had a secret weapon that he would unleash when the enemy was fully inside Germany. I partly believed it, it would have been dangerous to say it was not true.'

Martin Huneke was three and a half when Hitler came to power.

'People held a torch-lit procession through our village. I was so impressed by it that it stays my earliest memory. The fate of the Jews and others who disappeared from villages and towns was never made clear. I think most people thought they were forced to work and they were treated very harshly but I remember the shock after the war when we were informed of what had happened. We couldn't believe it. Perhaps it is a normal human habit to try and ignore misery and evil.

'There was a famous pianist in Germany and after a concert he spoke to his fans in the privacy of a café, saying he thought Hitler could never win the war and perhaps he shouldn't. One of the ladies there told the authorities and he was accused and killed. One heard stories about disappearances. Fear was everywhere.

The Hitler Youth came together three times per week, on Wednesday, Saturday and Sunday. We had a service – not a church service – but exercises of every kind, marching, shooting, singing Nazi hymns and learning speeches. Sometimes we went on a camp where we did the same thing but then for a week or so. For many it was very exciting. It disciplined you and taught you not to question.

In the first two years after 1939 I believed in it all but then I got more and more sceptical. I had to remain part of it but in the end I didn't obey them any more. I think the funniest thing was when we sang Mendelssohn and the Nazi leaders in the audience applauded and came to tell us it was a lovely song. We all knew it was forbidden because the composer was Jewish but no one told them the truth.

We looked on Nazis as buffoons.

In our school we were all of the same opinion and we were never reprimanded for it.

But we learned the art of hiding.

We knew to whom one had to speak the official language.

There was a strong feeling of guilt after the war and also a strong feeling of defensiveness. It is very difficult for people to admit that they went in the wrong direction for 15 years. I think those formative years made me strongly Christian.'

Victory

The red banner of the Soviet Union is flown from the top of the gutted Reichstag building by Russian soldiers.

CHAPTER TWELVE

VE-Day

'I am not moved to rush out tomorrow and wave a Union Jack in the village high street. I think it is a good sign that people are saying universally, "Our troubles are only just beginning"' *Maggie Joy Blunt, diarist*

On VE day ATS officer Molly Sale was among the crowds in London. 'We drew lots to decide who could have the evening off. I went up to London with one of the men from my company from Bedford. He had a three wheeler that he brought out of mothballs for the occasion. I got into the Buckingham Palace crowds. We all danced about, it was marvellous.'

Molly, who was 26 when war broke out, helped to organise transport for Eastern Command. Nevertheless, as an ambulance driver at the outbreak of war she saw some horrific sights, among them the return of the wounded from Dunkirk. (To gain her credentials as an ambulance driver, she had to drive with a glass of water in the back of the ambulance without spillage.)

As a lieutenant in the Auxiliary Territorial Service, Molly underwent a motorcycle instruction course and saw two of her female colleagues killed in crashes during tuition. However, the worst task that she recalls was being an officer compelled to accompany lorry loads of ATS girls to Saturday night dances at American air bases:

'You would not believe the trouble it was. I had to count girls into the lorry. By the time the last one came back you were five short again. I could see it from the girls' point of view, it was like being let out of school. They were given nylons, chocolates and everything else that our boys couldn't afford. They had far too much to drink. A lot of girls got into trouble and quite a lot of the Americans were already married.'

Mass Observation

Throughout the war and for some time afterwards more than 1,000 people in Britain were encouraged to keep diaries as part of an anthropological study known as the 'mass observation project' and from these we have an insight into some personal views about the end of the war.

One diarist, Maggie Joy Blunt, wrote on 4 May 1945:

'I am not moved to rush out tomorrow and wave a Union Jack in the village high street. I think it is a good sign that people are saying universally, "Our troubles are only just beginning", because it would be idiotic to assume they are over.'

Four days later another writer told how his family opened a tin of chicken bought in January 1941 to mark Peace Day. 'As

with many things it proved somewhat of a disappointment, for although it is genuine chicken – bones, skin and meat – it is spoilt by aspic jelly. Another long-cherished tin of sausages, purchased in November 1940, proved much more acceptable for lunch.'

The following day the same diarist recorded: 'Finished taking down black-outs at all windows and fanlights and parcelled them for storage in the loft, ready for the next war.'

Victory

London 8 May 1945: Crowds full of the spirit of VE day in Trafalgar Square celebrate the defeat of Hitler's armies and the end of the war in Europe.

Winning The Peace

As for the future, it was far from rosy. Germany was something of a blank canvas and while there was the promise of US money on the table to draw up a new nation, Stalin was poised in the wings to reap his war rewards. The destruction in France had mostly been wrought by the Allies in the last eleven months of the conflict. However, the country was running once again under its own steam with large tracts of its land untouched by the war. In

We Shall Remember

War memorial near Kemal Hill, Belgium. The bodies of nearly 12,000 British and Empire soldiers are here laid to rest.

the Low Countries the most pressing problem of starvation was being addressed. With the continent in chaos, Europeans were coming to terms with some of the greatest crimes ever known to man and the effects of the Holocaust would ripple on for generations. Within the midst of the liberated countries there were in varying numbers brave resistance fighters, malicious whistle-blowers and traitors. In fact, the political complexion of each remained as intricate and wide-ranging as it had been before the conflict began. It would be months or years before the rebuilding was completed, before the last refugee was returned home, before prisoners of war were repatriated, before the wounded were well again, before justice was done. And only then would a new age dawn, a chilly one, for the Cold War was just around the corner.

As for Britain and America, they were still at war in the east against Japan. Just as Hitler had refused to bow to the military might of the Allies, it seemed the Japanese were made of similar stuff. The killing would continue unabated for several months yet.

In America, before marking 13 May 1945 as a day of prayer, Harry S Truman made a formal declaration as follows:

'The Allied armies, through sacrifice and devotion and with God's help, have wrung from Germany a final and unconditional surrender. The western world has been freed of the evil forces which for five years and longer have imprisoned the bodies and broken the lives of millions upon millions of free-born men. They have violated their churches, destroyed their homes, corrupted their children and murdered their loved ones. Our Armies of

Liberation have restored freedom to these suffering peoples, whose spirit and will the oppressors could never enslave.
Much remains to be done. The victory won in the west must now be won in the east. The whole world must be cleansed of the evil from which half the world has been freed. United, the peace-loving nations have demonstrated in the west that their arms are stronger by far than the might of the dictators or the tyranny of military cliques that once called us soft and weak. The power of our peoples to defend themselves against all enemies will be proved in the Pacific war as it has been proved in Europe.'

Perhaps the last words belong to Churchill who had guided Britain for five turbulent years, by turns depressed and optimistic, elated and aghast. If his mood changed, his one avowed intention, to defeat Nazism and wipe it off the face of Europe, never did. At the end of hostilities, mindful of the threat from Japan and Russia and encapsulating the world as he saw it, he addressed the nation:

'I wish I could tell you tonight that all our toils and troubles were over. Then indeed I could end my five years' service happily, and if you thought that you had had enough of me and that I ought to be put out to grass I would take it with the best of grace. But, on the contrary, I must warn you as I did when I began this five years' task – and no one knew then that it would last so long – that there is still a lot to do and that you must be prepared for further efforts of mind and body and further sacrifices to great causes if you are not to fall back into the rut of inertia, the confusion of aim and the craven fear of being great. You must not weaken in any way in your alert and vigilant frame of mind. Though holiday rejoicing is necessary to the human spirit, yet it must add to the strength and resilience with which every man and woman turns again to the work they have to do, and also to the outlook and watch they have to keep on public affairs. . .
We seek nothing for ourselves. But we must make sure that those causes which we fought for find recognition at the peace table in facts as well as words, and above all we must labour to ensure that the World Organisation which the United Nations are creating at San Francisco does not become an idle name, does not become a shield for the strong and a mockery for the weak. It is the victors who must search their hearts in their glowing hours and be worthy by their nobility of the immense forces that they wield. . .
I told you hard things at the beginning of these last five years; you did not shrink and I should be unworthy of your confidence and generosity if I did not still cry: Forward, unflinching, unswerving, indomitable, till the whole task is done and the whole world is safe and clean.'

Index

Index